My Long Affair with Auntie

Aftim Kreitem

Clink Street

London | New York

Published by Clink Street Publishing 2016

Copyright © 2016

First edition.

ISBN: 978-1-911110-02-6
eISBN: 978-1-911110-03-3

Contents

Acknowledgements   1

Foreword   3

Chapter 1 – The Very Beginning   5

Chapter 2 – How My Career Started   12

Chapter 3 – My Broadcasting Journey   18

Chapter 4 – From Cyprus to England   23

Chapter 5 – Moving to Rhodes   25

Chapter 6 – Back to England and Buckingham Palace   30

Chapter 7 – The Golden Age   34

Chapter 8 – Changing the Name of the Station   38

Chapter 9 – The New Blood Policy   43

Chapter 10 – Back at the BBC   46

Chapter 11 – Radical Changes   51

Chapter 12 – Arab Sports Personality of the Year   55

Chapter 13 – Official Duty Tour   62

Chapter 14 – The Crucial Difference   65

Chapter 15 – The VIP Experience   68

Chapter 16 – The Television Experience   73

Chapter 17 – The Al-Jazeera TV Experience   77

Chapter 18 – Sharq Al-Adna Radio Station   88

My first time working in a radio station goes back to the early fifties in Sharq Al-Adna (Near East Arab Broadcasting Station) founded by Britain in Palestine in 1941 during the British Mandate.

My unexpected broadcasting career lasted over 60 years, mainly with the BBC Arabic Service. Here I provide, for the first time, an insight into the function of the Arabic Service. Despite having an illustrious career, stretching over 37 years with the BBC alone, I left this great organisation without a pension and not even a farewell cup of tea ... Why?

Acknowledgements

It would have been more appropriate if this book had been written immediately after leaving the BBC. But since the year 2000, my broadcasting career has moved from radio to television. It records the many unusual tales of my broadcasting career which I have never previously written about or talked about on air; such as how I managed to enter Buckingham Palace without an official permit; how an Arab general smashed his son's radio simply because he was listening to the BBC; and how when, on my initiative, the Arabic Service successfully organised and presented the first-ever Arab Sports Personality of the Year in Cairo. An Arab journalist wrote to say: "We learned at school that the British followed a policy of divide and rule, but now they want to unite us in sport." But topping all the unusual surprises was a generous gift from a royal prince.

My journey is a unique one: it began when I, as a young man, started out full of ambition, equipped only with a birth certificate and, despite setbacks and difficulties, succeeded in becoming a newsreader, programme producer, presenter, football and tennis commentator. This was achieved at a time when even to make an international telephone call a person was required to register twenty-four hours earlier.

This personal account of my career charts its development during what was known as the golden age of the Arabic Service, when the entire Arab world tuned their radios to the BBC for objective accounts of what was going on in the world, particularly in the Middle East. This golden age disappeared recently as a result of the spread of the satellite stations.

It may be the first time that readers in the UK and beyond and particularly the Arab world, receive inside knowledge about how the Arabic Service operated decades before Lord Hall, the Director-General of the BBC, said: "My aim is for the BBC to be the number one destination for talented people regardless of their background. It is time for action" (*Daily Telegraph,* 21 June 2014).

This great media organisation remains number one in the world. That assertion does, however, not overlook the fact that when you mow your grass in your garden, the mower does not stop for any beautiful plant in its way.

Foreword

As a Palestinian refugee who never lived in a camp but lived in three different countries – Cyprus for nine and half years, Rhodes, Greece for eighteen months and England for over fifty years – a frequent question I have faced, whenever I am introduced to anyone, is, "Where do you come from?" I was astonished when, on joining Bromley Cricket and Tennis Club in London in the early seventies and a member asked me the usual question, the following conversation ensued. I replied, "Palestine." He tried to confirm, "Pakistan?" I said, "No, Palestine." And then he asked, "Where is that?" Of course, he had never read the Bible nor attended a geography lesson – or perhaps he was a disguised Zionist!

For me one question that keeps resonating in my mind, even after so many years have passed since I left the BBC at the beginning of the twenty-first century, is the manner of my leaving. Professional friends of mine outside the BBC describe my treatment as 'disgraceful' when I tell them that I left this great organisation without a pension or even a cup of coffee to mark more than thirty-seven years of loyal and dedicated service, plus many more years as a correspondent in Cyprus for the Arabic Service. This was a flagrant discrimination against its own working terms and conditions. But as a result of this melodrama, I built a name for myself among many listeners and among certain quarters of the Arab press.

My long journey in broadcasting reveals countless unusual stories never aired before and tells the story of how my journey in broadcasting was realised.

I am most indebted to my wife Suzanne, for all her personal assistance during my work at the BBC and other media organisations, and also to my son Simon and daughter Melanie for their help in photography and printing in addition to have given us such wonderful grandchildren.

I also dedicate this book to my late brother Michael, who supplied me with copies of Sharq Al-Adna magazine which is now defunct and has disappeared without trace throughout the Middle East; also to my brother Hanna, who helped me start my broadcasting career. I would also like to dedicate my book to the rest of the family in Jordan and the West Bank, who became my own sort of audio research department, keeping me informed about the good reaction from listeners in the area. This all happened at a time before the mobile, email and the rest of modern technology. Last but by no means least, Joseph Raffoul, who assisted me with much technical advice.

Chapter 1
The Very Beginning

I boarded a Dakota plane from Qalandia Airport in Jerusalem, when it was operating before the 1967 war. I was on my way to Cyprus via Beirut, as there was no direct flight then, and had to stay one night in a five star hotel in the Lebanese capital at the expense of Middle East Airlines, which was an incentive for me to buy my return ticket at a cost of £23. The next day I continued on to Nicosia airport. Despite the fact that it was a Dakota two-engine plane no one felt comfortable – at that time there was a great fear of flying.

It was my first-ever experience of being on a plane. That was not strange in December 1953, as jet planes were not yet operating in the Middle East. As was the tradition in Jerusalem at that time, most of my family and friends had gathered at the airport to see me off. My mother had a very valuable piece of advice for me: "Look after yourself, son," she said, "and be aware of the girls there." I followed her advice seriously and disembarked from the plane at Nicosia International Airport with a sulky face. I was only eighteen years old. I did not have the slightest idea that this flight would herald the beginning of my broadcasting career in Arabic – even though my secondary education did not qualify me to enroll in this field. I went on to train as a studio manager. This was at a time when there were few radio stations, particularly in the Middle East.

So I started my broadcasting career as a technician in a

radio station called Sharq Al-Adna, learning how to record on to tapes and discs. Nowadays the job has been upgraded and is called "studio manager". I was there for the next three years. It was the start of nearly sixty years in broadcasting, the only career I have known. But the road to achieve it was, as expected, not without obstacles. Nevertheless, it was achieved with good response from the BBC Arabic Service listeners and even from certain Arab newspapers, as is illustrated by the following article written by Samir Junket, sports editor for the daily Jordanian paper *Al Rai*, under the title "Towards the Goal":

Aftim Kreitem The Complete Star:

نحو الهدف

أفتيم قريطم
النجم الشامل

● سمير جنكات

خلال مزاملته لاكرم صالح
ومرسى بشوتي وبعد
رحيلهما عن اذاعة؛ لكن
وائار الغانية، بقي
الاذاعي المعروف أفتيم
قريطم مصدر جذب
ومبعث الهام لكثير من
المستمعين الشباب، روج
لنجوم الرياضة
الانجليزية
وبانقصوص نجوم كرة
القدم، مانما روج لائدية
الانجليزية قسائهم في
انتشارها على مساحة
الوطن العربي وانتوا —
النجوم والاندية —
وكأنهم جزء من الوطن
العربي؛
في هذه الايام، كشف برنامج
جديد يقدمه قريطم ولا
علاقة له بالرياضة عن
قرب ولا من بعيد، حجم
المخزون الثقافي الذي
يمتله والذي وظفه طيلة
فترة عمله الاذاعي
لحدن المستمع — ايا
كانت ميوله — للبرنامج
الذي يقدمه.
يبرنامج «لحن وحنين»،
يستعرض قريطم فيه
معلومات موسيقية
مصحلة بمرافقة فقرات
ثقافية ومعلومات
مختلفة تدفع المستمع
لمتابعته حتى وان كان لا
يبالي باللحن ولا يملك
الحنين؛
تحية الرجل الذي لا تربطنا
به معرفة شخصية، على
الخدمات التي قدمها في
مجال الاعلام الرياضي،
ودعاؤنا له بالتوفيق
على الدوام.

During his work with the late Akram Saleh and Mosa Bishouty the well-known broadcaster Aftim Kreitem inspired and attracted many listeners from among the youth to the sports world of Britain, especially the world of footballers and the English clubs. He spread their popularity across the Arab world, making people feel as if they were part of it. These days a new programme – nothing to do with sport – presented by Aftim Kreitem showcases the breadth of the cultural knowledge that he has displayed throughout his career. Through his programme *Lahn Wa Haneen* (*Yearn for a Melody*) composed of music and general knowledge, including how certain customs originated and other interesting facts, he attracted listeners to the programme, even if they did not yearn for a particular piece of music. We salute the man, whom I personally have not met, for his work in the sports media. (11 August 2001)

I learnt about the article when, while visiting Amman on the eve of my nephew's wedding, a relative phoned my brother to say that I had been mentioned in *Al Rai* newspaper. My immediate reaction was to wonder why the journalist had chosen to write about me now, since I had left the BBC more than a year previously. Of course I was very pleased, and even more pleased to find my *Lahn Wa Haneen* series was repeated several times, even after I left the BBC on 15 September 2000.

The late Sheikh Fahd Al-Sabah, President of the Kuwait Football Federation, and Asian Olympic President, killed during the Iraq's invasion of Kuwait in 1990

Carlos Alberto, scored the goal in 1970 World Cup final, many consider it the greatest ever. It was the final goal in Brazil 4-1 rout of Italy. The picture taken when he was managing the Emirates National Football team during The World Cup Final in Italy 1990

Visiting Saudi Arabia to hear Prince Faisal describing the first Arab Sport Personality of the year as a noble cause

In Jeddah after tennis tournament in November 1994

An interview with the late Bobby Robson, Manager of England Football National Team

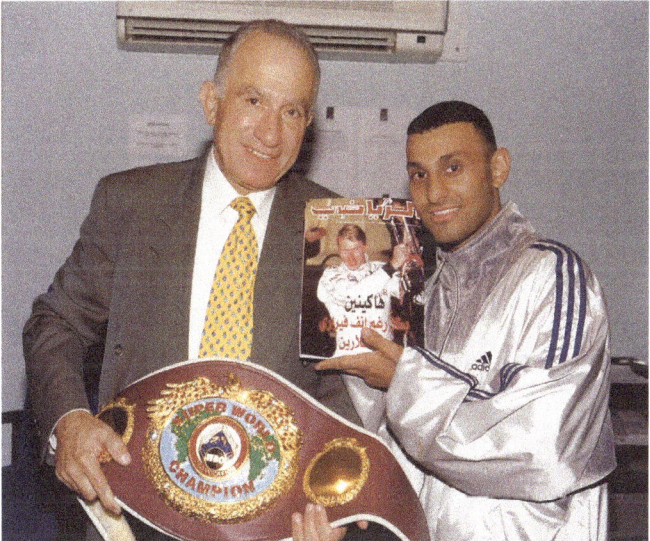

Prince Naseem Hamad wins his 3rd major title in super bantamweight

What had interrupted my education was the trouble in Palestine, as a result of which I did not attend any school for three years.

My first school was Omaria, located in a beautiful spot in Jerusalem, surrounded by trees as far as the eye could see. It was not far from the Jewish Montefiore settlement. Sometimes terrorists used to open fire on Arab areas and school would be interrupted. We lived in a beautiful, large house in the grounds of Clarisse Convent. Between our house and the Convent, there was a playing field, used by students from Frère College once a week, and it had two goalposts and proper markings for a football pitch. I and my brothers became very popular with boys from our neighborhood as we let them come through our house so that they could play football with us.

In return for this favour the nuns used to ask us to bring milk and their post to them from other convents in Jerusalem. To do this job, my brother Issa and I used to take either bus number 6 or 7. He was twelve years old, two years older than me. Bus number 7 used to pass in front of the Montefiore settlement which was situated on a hill. Every time we boarded a bus which passed below the settlement, we prayed and made the sign of the cross for our safety. The number 6 bus also used to pass in front of the King David Hotel. In July 1946 we narrowly escaped death as we were on a bus that passed the hotel just two minutes before the infamous explosion. In the bombing 92 people were killed, including British officers.

Two years later, we took refuge in the old city of Jerusalem, abandoning all our belongings in our home. We thought, like most Palestinians, that this would be a temporary measure lasting only a few weeks. Every now and then my father used to send me to check on the house we had temporarily left. The final time was on 14 May 1948, the last day of the British Mandate. After checking the house, I waited at length for the bus, but since there was no sign of it, I decided to walk towards an alternative bus stop. A bus arrived and I was lucky to board it. When I reached Jaffa Gate my father was there, waiting anxiously for me. He was right to be anxious as this would be the bus's last journey before the gate closed – and the gate remained closed for nineteen years, until Israel occupied Jerusalem and the rest of the West Bank during the 1967 war. I sometimes wonder what would have happened to me if I had not made that final bus journey as a teenage boy.

It would be two long decades until, during a visit to Jerusalem, I saw my old house again. Then I discovered, to my great surprise, that the long distance I had remembered between my house and school from nineteen years earlier, was actually very short – not more than a ten-minute walk. This is proof that when we are young we tend to see everything big.

Chapter 2
How My Career Started

My first job as studio manager came through my two brothers who were working as engineers in Sharq Al-Adna, known in English as the Near East Arab Broadcasting Station (NEABS), which had been founded in 1941 by the British. Very few people nowadays would have heard of it, despite its staggering rise from humble origins to become the pinnacle of radio stations throughout the Middle East – becoming so popular that, in the ears of its listeners, it achieved Hollywood status in the Arab World. It was located first in Palestine but was moved to Cyprus in 1948, at the end of the British Mandate in Palestine.

It was five years later, on 14 December 1953 to be exact, that I started my work in Sharq Al-Adna (NEABS). My first lesson was to learn how to dub and record programmes. Throughout the duration of this process, I did not utter one word, fearing that I would spoil the dubbing by implanting my voice on the recording. In the space of a few months I was able to master the job to a very high standard, and was able even to assist producers in choosing suitable music for a particular theme. That dubbing included songs by Fairuz, a well-known Lebanese singer, who became famous partly as a result of her records being played by this station on a powerful medium wave throughout the Arab world, contributing to her being able to establish herself as a leading star and talented singer.

Well known broadcaster at the time Taghreed Al-Hussainy in studio of Sharq Al-Adna 1955

Well known Broadcaster at the time Taghreed Al-Hussainy in studio of Sharq Al-Adna in Limassol.

In late October 1956, the staff at the station in Limassol were surprised when a notice appeared on the noticeboard calling for a general staff meeting. A few hours later it was removed but it reappeared two weeks later. There were two reasons why the meeting was delayed: the first was a small-scale attack carried out by Israel near Hebron; the second was much more serious, since Israeli forces were advancing towards the Suez Canal.

The meeting took place at the the station's club, in the centre of Limassol, and was attended by most of the staff. Mr Ralf Poston, the Head of NEABS, who chaired the meeting, began by asking the staff to switch on the radio in the hall at 5 pm local time (3 pm GMT) and listen to the station, as one of our colleagues was due to read an ultimatum that Britain and France had issued against Egypt. The announcement made it clear that, with immediate effect, the station would have a new name: "Voice of Britain".

رالف بوستن

Ralph Poston
The Managing Director of NEABS

Mr Poston tried to calm the staff's fears by saying that this was a temporary arrangement, and he hoped that the new name Voice of Britain would last for only a short time and the famous radio station would soon be revived. The staff for their part, asked him to broadcast over the radio that they were working under duress. In fact, it was I who recorded that message. But as soon as it was aired, Mr Poston and his wife were put under house arrest until they were forced to go back to England.

While Voice of Britain – engaged in a propaganda campaign against President Nasser of Egypt – was desperately seeking to employ any person ready to broadcast in Arabic, I refused to seize the opportunity to become a broadcaster.

After a brief period of showing solidarity with many of my colleagues, mostly those working on the programming side, I resumed my work as a studio manager.

One month before Voice of Britain closed down in March 1957, on my own initiative I recorded, narrated and produced a programme on tape, which I called *Voices I Heard from Sharq Al-Adna*. I was twenty-one years old at the time. This recording is the only archive left from Sharq Al-Adna. When BBC's Radio 4 made a documentary on the historic role played by Sharq Al-Adna in the Middle East, they used extracts from my programme.

B B C

BRITISH BROADCASTING CORPORATION
BROADCASTING HOUSE
LONDON W1A 1AA
TELEPHONE 071 580 4468
TELEX 265781
CABLES: BROADCASTS LONDON

Aftim Kreitem
room 411 Centre Block
Bush

direct dial: 081-765 5708

13 September 1994

Dear Aftim

SUEZ: *The Propagation of Truth*

This is just to thank you very much for your splendid contribution to this programme, and a reminder that it goes out on Thursday, 15 September at 7.20 pm on Radio Four.

Thank you also for supplying us with the excellent Sharq archive material. I hope your cassette arrived safely. Please could you also pass on my thanks to your colleague who helped us with the Patriotic Egyptian music.

It was a pleasure to meet you and I hope our paths cross again soon. I think someone should make a film about Sharq and the Voice of Britain!

With all best wishes,

Yours sincerely

Nigel

Nigel Acheson

Senior Producer
Arts, Science and Features, Radio

Nigel Acheson letter 9

I do not think that, even after my long broadcasting career, I could have produced a better programme. After I had finished making my programme, all the recordings and the archived programmes stored in the library had been destroyed by order of the Foreign Office.

The Voice of Britain had taken over all the transmitters of NEABS and shared them with the BBC, including its Arabic Service. However, the Eden's government was becoming increasingly impatient about what it regarded as the BBC's disloyal attitude and it came under increasing pressure to defend its impartiality at home and abroad. For its part, the BBC considered itself compromised as a result of its association for a brief period with the government propaganda on Voice of Britain and it having shared the transmitters left from Sharq Al-Adna. But the BBC won the battle of protecting its charter. After Eden's resignation and the closing down of Voice of Britain early in 1957, the transmitters were used only to relay the BBC's external services including the Arabic Service.

Sharq Al-Adna is covered adequately in Chapter 18.

I was moved, along with the rest of the technical staff, to the transmitter site in Zighy about 15 miles from Limassol. My job there entailed tuning various radio receivers to BBC frequencies.

It was a very boring job, apart from occasionally having to make announcements to apologise to the listeners when reception deteriorated, before playing emergency programmes from the relay station.

In order to alleviate the boredom, I made myself busy by recording the English and Arabic news bulletins, which were the same in content as they were broadcast from the World Service and the Arabic Service of the BBC. This helped me not only to improve my English but also to learn how to translate the news into Arabic, a task which prompted me to revise my Arabic grammar. The development of these skills led eventually to me becoming an announcer, presenter, producer, and football and tennis commentator.

Aftim tuning radios

Chapter 3
My Broadcasting Journey

My work as studio manager entailed not only recording on to tapes and discs, but also editing out whole words, and even single letters, in a very skilful way so that no listener would be able to notice the editing. And all this was done in the old-fashioned way using a blade and joining tape, rather than the modern easy digital way. The modern technological advancements are like a miracle when you think back to the facilities we had in the old days.

At that time, even to make an international telephone call you had to book it twenty-four hours in advance. This my brothers and I had to do when, while living in Cyprus, we received a cable from a cousin in Jerusalem saying "father passed away". We booked an international telephone call not knowing whether it was our father or our cousin's father who had died, and we had a long, anxious wait before we were able to discover that our father was alive and well.

My work as studio manager lasted for three years until NEABS closed down during the Suez Crisis in 1956.

The size of a tape recorder BTR2 was more than one metre high.

Author using BTR2 tape recorder

My first attempt to become a broadcaster came as a result of my own initiative: on hearing the news that Archbishop Makarios was to be released from his exile in the Seychelles, I took my own Grundig audio tape recorder to a main street in Limassol, plugged it in in one of the shops, and started to record and comment on the celebration that was taking place. I sent the tape to the BBC Arabic Service and, to my great surprise, it was broadcast as part of the newsreel and I was credited as their correspondent in Cyprus – when I heard that, I could not believe my ears.

Much wider celebrations were due to be held on 1 March when Makarios arrived back in Nicosia and I was officially asked to cover the event. But all my hard work on that particular day went in vain, as I had not understood what the editor had meant when he had instructed me to send the tape by 'air freight'. I was disappointed when my report was not aired, because I had sent the tape by airmail and it had not arrived in time. As a result of that experience, I started to dispatch all tapes by going to Nicosia airport and arranging for them to be put on board the first plane flying to London – a far cry from the transmitters and telephone lines that are used nowadays. Using this method, the reports arrived in time to be broadcast in the evening newsreel.

On 13 December 1959 Archbishop Makarios was elected President of Cyprus and, from then on, many Arab delegations began to visit Cyprus, opening up the opportunity for me to cover their visits with both reports and interviews. This culminated in a private interview with President Makarios, conducted in English, for the BBC Arabic Service. Taking the tape of the interview to the relay station, I edited, translated and voiced it, before having it put on board the first plane flying to London. These opportunities strengthened my relationship with the Arabic Service as their correspondent in Cyprus.

BRITISH BROADCASTING CORPORATION
MIDDLE EAST OFFICE

WAZZAN BLDG.
PHOENICIA ROAD
BEIRUT
P. O. B. 3509
CABLES : BROADCASTS BEIRUT   TEL. Nos.   25658
                                                 23102

15th March 1961

Dear Mr. Kreitem,

I have heard from London that the following items from you were used in "Round the World" during February :-

1. Interview with President Makarios on Cypriot relations with the Arab World

2. Interview with U.A.R. Ambassador to Cyprus

3. Carnival in Limassol

I am, therefore, arranging for the equivalent of fifteen guineas sterling to be transferred to your account with Barclays Bank Ltd., D.C. & O., Limassol, in payment of our fee for these. When the money has been received, will you please sign the enclosed receipt over the stamp and return it to this Office.

Yours sincerely,

(H.F. Duckworth)
Middle East Representative.

Mr. Aftim E. Kreitem,
P.O. Box 219,
LIMASSOL,
C Y P R U S .

Letter confirming the interview with President Makarios

Aftim Kreitem prior to boarding the military plane

One of the most frightening reports I ever made was on a British air manoeuvre which took place at one of its bases in Cyprus early in the sixties. A huge tank was due to be dropped from the air and I boarded a military plane to witness it. When the time for the manoeuvre arrived, the pilot asked me to descend the stairs so that I could observe the drop more closely. Minutes later, when the order came and the tank started its descent, I found myself hanging in mid-air as the huge aircraft doors remained opened. It was only with great difficulty that I succeeded in climbing back up to the cockpit. Nevertheless, that was a minor experience when compared to the one endured by my colleague George Stivaros, who was a freelance photographer with Pathé News. He had been given the job of filming paratroopers jumping out of a plane. When the fifty-five paratroopers had jumped, he had found himself alone in the plane with the doors still open! He later admitted to me that he was so terrified that he wet himself.

From 1959 to early 1963, as well as my work for the Arabic Service, I continued to work at the relay station. There were several other Palestinians also working there; the rest of the staff were British or Greek Cypriots. Some of them tried unsuccessfully to take our jobs, even appealing to President Makarios, but he refused their request. But one day in February 1963, we awoke to the terrible news that one of our Palestinian colleagues had been shot dead at his home. Late the previous night there had been a knock at the door and he had got up out of bed to answer it and his wife had heard him speak the name of one of his work colleagues. This happened at a time when IOKA was actively fighting for the independence of Cyprus. Arriving immediately at the scene of the crime, a Turkish Cypriot policeman had followed the car of the assailant, but when he had reached the man's house, he had been told that he was sleeping. Before going to wake the man up, he had checked the car engine and discovered it was very hot, unlike his bed which was cold. This evidence was, however, not enough to convict the murderer. The other Palestinian staff at the relay station were so shocked by what had happened that they all submitted their resignations.

Chapter 4
From Cyprus to England

As I am holding a British passport, I opted to seek work in England, arriving in London in the early morning of 23 June 1963. A few hours later, my brother Hanna and I were queuing outside Wimbledon, waiting to enter this famous complex to watch the stars of the tennis world at that time.

The next day, I went to Bush House to visit a number of broadcasters with whom I had worked at Sharq Al-Adna in Cyprus and who had followed my work as a correspondent in Cyprus. One of them found work for me as an outside contributor for the Arabic Service.

A more unusual opportunity presented itself when one of the producers invited me to take part in a play in which some famous Arab actors were performing. The producer made me attend daily rehearsals just to say the line, "Who is at the door, sir?" I practiced that line for five days in the studio, brushing shoulders with several leading Egyptian film stars, including Youssef Wahbe, and was paid 12 guineas. The producer insisted on crediting my name among those of the famous stars. Since my first name was not Arabic, he changed it from Aftim to Said. That was the only time I ever took part in acting – if one can call it acting.

So for my first eighteen months in London I worked as an outside contributor for the Arabic Service, taking part in programmes such as *World at One*, *World at Six* and various sports programmes. Since I was not a member of staff, I was not allowed to read a news bulletin. I supplemented my income by working occasionally with the Central Office of Information (COI) as an interpreter and liaison officer for Arab dignitaries visiting England. Before I had worked in these roles, I had stood in queues to visit the House of Commons. But with the COI job I visited this historic place and many other London landmarks in style by official car.

My income was about £20 a week. I was advised that if I went to a bank someone would assist me with my income tax. At that time, I had an account at Barclays Bank in Trafalgar Square (no longer in existence) and so I made my way there to enquire if they had a section that would help me with my income tax. The answer was yes, as I had £2000 in a provident fund I had opened while working in Cyprus. Taking down my details, the clerk asked me where I worked. My answer was the BBC. When, a few days later, I attended the appointment, to my great surprise I was led to a big conference room, where three executives were waiting for me. I apologised immediately and said that I was certainly in the wrong place, as I was not Robin Day, a very famous broadcaster in the UK at that time.

Chapter 5
Moving to Rhodes

In the meantime I sat for two examinations, one to join the Arabic Service and the other for Voice of America in Rhodes, Greece, and it was the latter which accepted me first. The contract was for one year only, with the possibility of an extension.

On my first day of work in Rhodes, I was given a news bulletin to read five minutes before going on air. This was very different to the BBC where you are given ample time to prepare to ensure that you get the Arabic grammar exactly right. When I came out of the studio I was greeted with big smiles from my new colleagues. A month later I was asked to host the breakfast show, a two-hour live programme based on reading news and introducing reports interspersed with western music. The rest of the day was spent preparing for the next morning's show.

In late February 1966, I was sitting with my colleague Peter Zabaneh in a coffee shop near the seafront in Rhodes when he suddenly stood up from the table and rushed over to welcome a man I did not recognise , as television had not yet reached that part of the world. However, when I was introduced to him, I immediately knew he was the eminent Dr Munif Al-Razzaz. His name was well known throughout the Arab world as he was the political successor to Michel Aflaq, founder of the Ba'ath party. He had arrived in Rhodes the night before, following a coup d'état which had taken place in Syria on 23 February 1966, deposing him and the President Mr Adib Al-Hafez. We invited him to have dinner with us. My colleague suggested a remote restaurant in the middle of a forest. Since the night before as part of a news bulletin I had read a report about the assassination of Mr Shishakly, a former Syrian President, at a remote restaurant in Argentina, I tried to suggest somewhere a bit closer, but my colleague persuaded our eminent guest to have dinner with us in the remote restaurant. We enjoyed his company very much as he was a man of supreme intellect. In the days that followed we spent our spare time showing him various places on the island and learning from him about his experiences in Arab politics. An eye-opener for me in regard to how certain Arab leaders work in secret came when he bought a copy of *The Economist* and I asked him why he had chosen that particular magazine. To my surprise he replied that matters that he and his fellow leaders had discussed in Syria behind closed doors, had been published soon after in that magazine. I invited Mr Al-Razzaz to stay at my apartment while I was away on a trip to England. That was the last contact I had with this highly intellectual man. I never disclosed what he told me to the famous magazine.

Programme production at the Voice of America radio station was not as impressive as at the Arabic Service, which at that time was like a mini-BBC Radio 4. During my work at the relay station in Cyprus I had been an avid listener to the service. Most of those colleagues in Rhodes were brilliant translators. From time to time some of the senior staff used to gather around a tape recorder and listen to their voices with great joy, as if they themselves were novices.

During the summer, I invited my parents to visit me in Rhodes, which they enjoyed very much, particularly my father, who loved to stay on the beach for long periods of time watching the beautiful Swedish girls in their bikinis. No wonder, then, that he and my mother brought ten of us into the world, seven boys and three girls! I am number five. My father was a talented carpenter, but he was only able to earn a modest income from this trade. When times were tough, he gave up his work as a carpenter to open a souvenir shop or to rear pigs – despite it being an activity that it is contrary to the religion of both Jews and Muslims. During the Second World War, since there were so many British troops stationed in Palestine, the rearing of pigs became a very prosperous business. When towards the end of the war he and his partners started to lose money, he returned to carpentry, with its very modest income. When things deteriorated even further, we had to take refuge in the old city of Jerusalem where we lived in one large, long room. After struggling there for a while, we moved temporarily to Amman. That very evening we heard that the room we had been living in in Jerusalem had been bombed.

My father refused to tolerate a practice which was common at that time amongst merchants in Amman in lieu of cash payment: in exchange for the manufacture of doors and windows for their new buildings, they would ask him to throw a stone and the distance it reached would be his land. He viewed this practice as strange and, unfortunately, he would not accept it – he wanted cash for food.

It is my mother who must take most of the credit for bringing us all up to love each other. This she achieved without the modern comforts of life, like a dishwasher and washing machine, which she did not enjoy until late in her life. During her visit to Rhodes, she used to get up as early as three in the morning to prepare breakfast for me and see me off to work. Her mother lived to over ninety, and was greatly loved by all her grandchildren. She was a very well-known and well-loved figure whenever she walked the streets of Jerusalem and beyond. On one occasion she even went as far as Beirut to see a granddaughter without knowing her address, but luckily, while walking in the centre of Beirut, she accidentally bumped into one of her grandsons and he told her where to go.

My mother had one sister – sadly my grand mother all thirteen of her siblings had died very young because of a weakness in breast-feeding. My mother and her sister survived through having a wet nurse, whom, throughout their lives, they welcomed to their home in Jerusalem. One thing my mother never told us was that, following their father's sudden death, her mother had had to work as a nanny to bring up her and her sister – despite the fact that, as I discovered only recently through reading a book, my grandfather was one of the richest farmers in Jericho, Palestine. As she had two daughters and no sons to inherit, she never benefitted from any of his wealth. Sadly this unjust practice still prevails in the Arab world, which favours boys at the expense of girls.

One month before the end of my contract with Voice of America, the head of the station, Mr Cochran, spoke to me about extending my contract for two more years, and arrangements were made for me to sign it at the American Embassy in London, where I had signed my first contract. Three weeks later there was a dramatic and sudden change at the station. Mr Cochran was ordered to go back to the USA and was replaced by a new boss called Mr Baker, who suddenly asked to meet me, without giving a reason. When the meeting took place at the Rhodes Hotel, he told me bluntly that there would be no contract extension – no reason was given. Of course I was shocked to hear this bad news, especially as it was only one week before my wedding day in London. In fact, on arriving back at the office, a colleague in the Newsroom shouted across to me that he had received a wedding invitation from London and, to my great surprise, it was to my wedding. A parcel containing the other invitations for me to distribute arrived two days later.

After three sleepless nights, I decided to consider the three months' extension as an appropriate honeymoon in Rhodes, and so my lovely wife and I toured every part of the beautiful island. Then, at the end of March 1967, we set off by car on our long return journey to England, first boarding a ship to Piraeus in Athens. On board, we met up with some friends with whom we discussed our trip through Europe. They advised us not to go directly to Belgrade, but instead to go through Skopje – advice which, regrettably, we followed.

After a few hours on very rough roads, we lost our way. We stopped several times, asking anyone we met on the road for directions, but we couldn't find anybody who could understand either English or Greek, and my smattering of Italian did not get us very far. But, to my great surprise, when in frustration and despair I uttered one word in Arabic, a man standing nearby asked, "Do you understand Arabic?" He directed us to a small village, but when we reached it, the people stared at us as if we were from outer space. We managed to find a small place to stay, but, having spent an uncomfortable night, we left early in the morning.

Unfortunately, at that point we found that our already difficult journey became even more difficult! We came across two broken bridges and were forced to wait for hours until they were temporarily repaired. Eventually we left Yugoslavia, as it was then called, and entered Austria, but there had been heavy snow and we passed many cars better than our Ford Taunus that had been left stranded at the side of the road. Our route inevitably took us up a very high mountain. We succeeded in reaching the top where we rested for a while before facing the problem of how to descend on the icy roads without having any chains on our wheels. Almost immediately after resuming our journey, I lost control of the car, which began to skid dangerously towards the side of the road and a deep ravine. Miraculously I managed to steer the car out of the skid towards the other side of the hill where we came to a halt. A car going in the opposite direction, which did have chains on its wheels, stopped to make sure we were OK, and the driver gave us the very good advice not to use the brake but instead to rely on the handbrake. I and my pregnant wife had had a narrow escape.

Chapter 6
Back to England and
Buckingham Palace

We continued our adventure, travelling through Germany and Belgium, and arriving in London before seven in the morning of 7 May 1967. By one o'clock that very same day I was taking part in the *World at One* programme for the Arabic Service! The nightmare of work instability ended as I was able to resume my work as an outside contributor for the service until I could sit the BBC examination again and become a permanent member of staff. In fact, the written examination turned out to be so difficult that when it was over I couldn't think straight and I couldn't find my way out of the building in which it had been held. Then it was back to Bush House for the oral exam, which was relatively easy in comparison. Another difficulty was filling in the application form for the post, which required me to name any degree or college certificate. Fortunately the name of my school helped me to disguise my lack of qualifications as it was called Terra Sancta College. Not having been to university was in my mind a disability, although later I came across several senior Corporation executives who had equally not enjoyed the advantage of higher education.

While I was waiting for the result of the exam, the Central Office of Information (COI) gave me the job of accompanying the entourage of King Faisal of Saudi Arabia during his state visit to Britain in May 1967, for three days of which he was the guest of the Queen at Buckingham Palace. Accompanying the King as part of his entourage was a man called Mr Nasser, who was the chief announcer at the Saudi Arabia radio station and a confidant of the King. Every day an official car would take him to Broadcasting House, so that he could file his morning and evening reports to his country, and I would accompany him. One day, on finishing his work at Broadcasting House, he insisted on being taken to the palace to meet King Faisal. No matter what I said, he would not accept that this was not possible since he didn't have an official permit to enter the palace – unlike in his own country where anybody can ask for a meeting with the King. He was so insistent that in the end I had no alternative but to ask the driver to raise the two flags of the UK and Saudi Arabia and try to enter the palace. Luckily Mr Nasser was wearing his national dress, and as soon as we approached the main gate of the palace the guard saluted us and we cruised past him up to the main entrance. I stepped out of the car to meet the butler and explained to him the situation, and he not only very warmly welcomed us, but took us on a tour of the palace including the banquet room, before showing the chief announcer to King Faisal's suite. This happened in May 1967 before the IRA started its bombing campaign and one month before the break-out of the Seven-Day War in the Middle East.

Earlier than expected, I received a letter from the BBC informing me that I had passed the examination and offering me the job of programme assistant, so my dream of becoming a professional broadcaster was on its way to being fulfilled. Despite proving myself eminently capable of carrying out my job as programme assistant – the official job title of an announcer – my broadcasting career, up to my retirement from the BBC in 2000, did not prove to be an easy road, although I did later learn how popular my name had become in certain parts of the Arab world.

Aftim in front of the BBC microphone

At that time the Arabic Service had 10 million daily listeners and was the largest station in the world after the English World Service, which used to broadcast from Bush House in thirty-eight languages. My first job had involved reading the news, doing continuity work and taking part in various programmes. Now, instead of translating news bulletins and dispatches, I was asked to present a very popular programme called *Western Listeners' Request*. Each week thousands of letters would arrive at Bush House from various parts of the Arab world, and my wife, son and daughter would help me to sort through them. A secretary would collect the chosen discs from the music library, and then I would carry them to the studio, with a running order, which I would hand to the studio manager before entering the studio to record the programme. When it was time to play a record, I would signal by waving my hand at him or her, and if editing was required, I would do it myself. In the BBC Home Service, such programmes would have the assistance of a producer and maybe also an editor.

Chapter 7
The Golden Age

The seventies and eighties were recognised as the golden age of the Arabic Service. It was a mini Radio 4 – I say 'mini' because we were broadcasting for nine hours a day. Nevertheless, the Service used to broadcast serious programmes on a broad range of subjects including culture, medicine, science and current affairs – with its programmes *World at One* and *World at Six*, and its coverage of the conferences of the Conservative, Labour and Liberal parties – in addition to sport, including live broadcast of the FA Cup Final and the League Cup Final from Wembley.

Mr Said al-Issa, who headed the Arabic Service Culture Unit, wrote an article in the well-known Saudi weekly magazine *Almajallah* to mark the occasion of the fiftieth anniversary of the BBC Arabic Service. He had given thirty years' service in the Arabic Service, having also worked as Head of Radio Jordan and Senior Editor of the Near East Arab Broadcasting Station. In his article published in the 10-16 February 1988 edition, he stated, "The achievement of the Arabic Service was great and remarkable." Despite the fact that it only transmitted for nine hours daily, it used to receive nearly 70,000 letters annually. Many people in the Arab world preferred to listen to the Arabic Service rather than their state-controlled stations, which concentrated on giving news about what their kings, presidents or rulers had been doing during the day, going from one place to another, whereas listening to the BBC they could hear real news.

A few months after joining the BBC I was asked to write, present and produce an additional programme called *Round About*, replacing a colleague who had had to take six months' sick leave. I very much enjoyed writing, presenting and producing this programme, which comprised a mixture of anecdotes and Arabic songs chosen to suit a particular subject. After the six months were up I continued for a further six months since the previous presenter had not been permitted to take any more sick leave and had been forced to retire. Instead of being in his "sick bed", he was in fact running a private translation company and when he failed to find another excuse he submitted his resignation. He showed me the letter he received from Charles Curran, the Director General at that time, expressing regret at his resignation after his many years of "loyal service". At the same time as presenting this programme, I was still reading the news and producing *Round the Arab World* (the western listeners' request programme) as well as taking part in various other programmes.

By this time I had completed one year at the Arabic Service as I had started work in June 1967 and by August 1968 was expecting, as was the normal practice, to be given a permanent post. But, despite having been locally recruited and holding a British passport, the BBC declined to give me a permanent post, with a retirement pension, which was against their own terms and conditions of service, according to "BBC REGULATIONS AND GENERAL INFORMATION FOR STAFF 4.3 PROBATIONARY PERIODS AND CONFIRMATION : The appointment of full-time and part-time staff is normally subject to a probationary period of one year. On completing their probationary period to the full satisfaction of the BBC in work and conduct, and provided that their health is considered satisfactory, they will be confirmed in their appointments. Those who fail to reach the standards required cannot expect to remain at the BBC's service. On being confirmed in their appointments all pensionable staff aged 21 or over are required to join the New Pension Scheme. Staff who are not already members of the New Pension Scheme, and who fail to complete the contribution form sent to them when they are due for confirmation will have pension contributions deducted, from their salary automatically at the lower rate."

That was different for staff recruited from outside the UK. The person with the power of 'discretion' to transfer an employee to a permanent post was the Head of the Arabic Service, who himself had no knowledge of the Arabic language. Instead, I was offered a contract for three years. The Arabic Service had seven alternating heads during my service. The first one who refused to follow the BBC rules of work was the same person who told me once, when I was working as a freelancer, to go and find work outside the BBC!

From time to time, we used to invite special guests to our sports magazine ALMAJAlA Alriaddiah which was very popular in the Arab World. One day I took the opportunity to invite her royal highness Princess Haya Bint Alhussain to Bush House to talk about her enthusiasm and love for sport, and she was dedicated and enthusiastic to horse riding, especially riding horses out in the desert and camping under the stars. She was given her first Arabian mare when she was 6 years old, and by the time she was 12, she became the youngest rider to ever represent her country in international competitions, and the first female to participate in the Royal Jordanian horse jumping team. Most unfortunate is that this popular sports magazine ceased to exist in the Arabic Service programmes

Her Royal Highness Princess Haya with author

Chapter 8
Changing the Name
of the Station

Nowadays broadcasting is much easier than it was in those days, due to the advancement of technology and digital transmission, and not having to rely too much on short wave transmission. Back then we had our own broadcasting etiquette, which meant that in the early morning we did not play songs about the moon, or talk about unpleasant subjects, like vomiting and death, when listeners were having their breakfast. Instead of Google searches and the many means available via modern technology nowadays, doing our research for specific material for certain programmes was not easy, and we had to rely on newspaper cuttings, available in Bush House library. We had more freedom in our production work, writing, producing, and presenting both live and recorded programmes ourselves.

I in particular enjoyed more freedom than others when producing and presenting sports programmes. The reason for this was that all my rather academic colleagues in the Arabic Service were not interested in playing or practicing sports. It was commonly thought in the Arab world that those people who failed to do their jobs properly in the news and current affairs departments were transferred to the sports department, unlike our counterpart commentators working for the UK stations who are admired and paid high salaries. So my enthusiasm for playing tennis regularly, and occasionally golf, helped me to find the right Arabic words for many of the technical sports terms which originated in English.

I also enjoyed writing, presenting, and producing special programmes, including *In London This Week* and *Messages from Arabs Living in England to their Families in the Arab World*. The latter was very popular, as Skype and mobile phones were not yet in use. I also enjoyed producing the special Christmas programmes every year. Most of my colleagues were university graduates who excelled in reporting the news and producing current affairs programmes, often having to translate reports into Arabic. Reading the news bulletins was entrusted to selected announcers. My interest in music and special programmes went back to my time working as a studio manager in Cyprus, when I became familiar with the technical aspects of how a studio works.

There is no doubt that the BBC is not just a great organisation but undeniably the best media organisation in the world. Despite its great name, however, one cannot close one's eyes to mistakes made by certain individuals, particularly in the Arabic Service, which Mr Said al-Issa also commented on in his article celebrating the BBC's fiftieth anniversary. He wrote: "Despite its great achievements, there were unfruitful instances committed by English officials, who called themselves Arabists, which suggested they were fluent in the Arabic language, but in reality most of them could hardly speak, apart from a few words."

In my opinion, one of the biggest-ever mistakes in the history of the Arabic Service was made by the Head of the Service in the early nineties when he changed the name, which had been very popular since its birth in 1938, to 'This is the BBC', although, to be fair to him, he did consult with the staff before implementing the change. We used to say in Arabic, "*Hona London*" ("This is London of the British Broadcasting Corporation"). As a result of this change, many Arab listeners confused our station with a new station called MBC, which was founded in London in 1992 by the Saudis. So the original name used daily for over sixty years disappeared from the air waves.

During this 'golden age' of the Service the staff were more creative. This was because the hours of transmission in those days were much shorter – nine hours a day compared to the present 24-hour service which means that staff have to work much longer hours. In my day the dawn transmission was only two hours. There was a dormitory hall where those of us working on the early morning programme could book a bed for the night. However, there was only a very thin curtain separating each of the thirty-eight beds and this lack of privacy created problems. On one occasion, for example, a French announcer, so incensed by the loud snoring of a colleague in the Arabic Service, jumped out of his bed and bit his big toe, in an attempt to stop his snoring – fortunately the disagreement was resolved without a fight. This dormitory hall does not exist anymore because Bush House was closed down and the staff moved to Broadcasting House. But my career in this building lasted over thirty-seven years. The luckiest of those years was 1964 – forty-eight years ago – when I met my wife-to-be in the BBC canteen.

Unlike nowadays, entering the building was very easy – there were no restrictions at all. Inside the building there were many studios. These were shared by all the external services' staff, but they had to be booked in advance. On rare occasions a section would overrun its session, but if this occurred, it used to be sorted amicably. The Arabic Service had its own permanent continuity studio. The Newsroom was in a very large hall where subeditors sat together with various translators and announcers. One day I was helping the main Arabic translator when a news item was placed in my hand. Its source was the United Nations and it concerned statements made by Mr Herzog, the Israeli ambassador, and Mr Shoqairy, the Palestinian representative. In it reference was made to Mr Herzog having said so and so. In contrast, when referring to statements made by the Palestinian the word 'claimed' was used. I stood up and said that since we worked in an impartial organisation, we shouldn't differentiate between the two speakers in this way. Five minutes later the subeditor agreed to alter the word 'claimed' to 'said'. It was very rare for translators to challenge subeditors, although I did hear of one occasion when an Arab announcer asked the English subeditor how it came to be that, in the intro of a news bulletin, the Israelis were reported to be 100 miles away from the Suez Canal, while in the detail of the report the distance became 190 miles! Of course, among the staff there were Zionist sympathisers as well as Palestinians. Michael Elkins, the BBC Middle East correspondent from 1965–83, admitted in a letter to the editor of *The Times* newspaper that he was a Zionist. Despite this admission, his reports were translated and read without any change on the *World at One* and the *World at Six* programmes on the Arabic Service. An exception was, however, made when he referred to Palestinians as 'mad dogs' in one of his reports following an explosion. But the weapon of impartiality prevails. I do know that an Arab colleague's contract was terminated when, while reading a press review, he referred to the *Daily Telegraph* as a Zionist paper.

During the Six-Day War in 1967, the Arab staff were shocked to hear that Jerusalem had fallen to the Israelis. All the announcers had a meeting with the Head of the Service, claiming that there was bias reporting. When he asked them to provide a source to substantiate this claim, they began to quote the Jordanian Ambassador in London. That denial lasted three days, in the face of television pictures showing Israeli tanks rolling into Jerusalem.

On 21 April 1996 the BBC Arabic Service launched a television news channel, via the Orbit channel owned by the Saudi Khalid Ben Abdullah, on condition that editorial matters were the full responsibility of the BBC. Only two years later Orbit Channel pulled the plug on the BBC Arabic TV Channel, immediately after it started to broadcast an episode of *Panorama* which was critical of Saudi Arabia. But in March

2008 the Service was relaunched, this time by the BBC alone, as an online service broadcasting 24 hours a day, seven days a week, funded initially by a grant-in-aid from the Foreign Office. But on 1 April 2014 the external services began to be financed from the television licence fee. And, of course, it now faces stiff competition from various Arab satellite channels which did not exist during the golden days of the BBC Arabic Service.

Chapter 9
The New Blood Policy

Broadcasting to overseas listeners is not like broadcasting within a country: the newsreaders need to read the news bulletin at a slower pace for the benefit of short wave listeners. At the time of NEABS one daily news bulletin was read at dictation speed. Before the introduction of emails you didn't get an immediate reaction from listeners. The external services had an audience research department, through which letters from listeners, whether critical or appreciative, would be distributed to the announcers. But it is only when you travel in the area to which you are broadcasting and meet people face to face that you can really gauge people's opinion. As my family live in Jerusalem andAmman, I first of all began to get good feedback on my work from them and then later, as I began to travel to various Arab countries, I began to get a sense that my hard work was appreciated.

The response from some of my bosses, however, went in the opposite direction. Under what the BBC called their 'fresh blood' policy, the maximum contract awarded to short-term programme assistants, i.e. announcers, was five years. But for the first eleven years my contract continued to be extended, so it came as a complete shock to learn, in 1979, that, after all my years of loyal service, the BBC had decided not to renew my contract, using the pretext of this so-called 'fresh blood' policy, which was not applicable to most of the staff. I was given three months' notice.

So, determined not to change country for a third time, I started to think of what I could now do for a living, as a married person with an English wife and two children. I knew that many Arab officials visiting London were unable to receive the Arabic Service, as the transmitters were directed towards the Middle East. But, for these affluent listeners, there were special arrangements put in place by the BBC so that during their stay in London they could hear the Service through the telephone line and charge it on their expenses. Although in England at that time community broadcasting was prohibited in accordance with the 1949 Post Office Act, I considered opening a radio station using telephone line. My wife and I approached the Post Office in London and started negotiations with their officials with a view to opening an Arabic Radio Station in London based on using telephone line.

At our preliminary meetings no objections were raised. Meanwhile, a Senior Personnel Officer in the Arabic Service called me into his office several times, telling me that he was very worried about my future and, in fact, during the last meeting he had tears in his eyes when he was speaking to me. At this point I told him in confidence about my plan. Later on I discovered that, not trusting his own secretary, he had found another secretary and dictated to her all that I had told him in total confidence. After that the Post Office officials turned down my proposal. It was not until the late eighties that the Home Office started to consider allowing community radio stations to operate in the UK.

After my last day at work in 1978, what I did in fact do was to start the first monthly talking magazine on cassette, considered to be the first of its kind worldwide, under the name of *Al-Wassel* meaning in Arabic 'the arrival and the connecter'. It was professionally produced and there was really no difference in quality from a radio programme, except that it was recorded on cassette. With contributions from broadcasters and journalists, in each edition we covered political issues, especially regarding the Palestinian problem, as well as various other subjects, including culture, music and interviews with famous musicians. Sadly the questions we put to certain ministers or experts about the Palestinian problem back then are still being asked today, thirty five years after the magazine's closure. It generated income from subscriptions and commercial revenues, but only lasted two years. When it came to an end certain people expressed an interest in taking over the talking magazine, but I was not sure of their intentions and I was determined that it should continue to be produced along the same editorial lines that I had learned from the BBC.

Chapter 10
Back at the BBC

One day the telephone rang in my office and at the other end of the phone was Emil Abdul Naby, an old colleague from the Music section at the Arabic Service, enquiring if I would be interested in presenting and producing the *Listeners' Request Programme* again. He offered me the sum of £80 weekly for two editions of the programme.

Back at Bush House after two years' absence, I was now inundated with work – in fact, more than I had ever had before – including various shifts opening and closing transmission and reading the news. I was given priority in producing and presenting the sports magazine programme. And, on top of that, I was also doing live football commentary. The Arabic Service had two regular slots: we broadcast a live football commentary for both the FA Cup Final and the League Cup Final. In addition, I was writing articles on sport for *Hona London*, a BBC publication similar to the *Radio Times*. My first opportunity to do TV football commentary had come after my eleven-year contract with the BBC had ended. The Football Association had offered me the opportunity to record a series of TV programmes called *The Road to Wembley*, with coverage from the third round of the FA Cup to the Final, which was live. I have also occasionally done live commentaries on TV international football matches and also live tennis from Wimbledon.

In radio recording it was common practice to mark any mistake for a repeat or to stop the recording to correct a mistake. I was once lectured by the producer Peter Di Palma when I stopped a recording ten minutes from the beginning to do a repeat. He was so annoyed that he shouted at me angrily, saying that the stoppage cost him a lot of money, because the dubbing was not only in Arabic but also in a number of other languages. I did not repeat that terrible mistake.

ENTERTAINMENT
LIMITED

ATV HOUSE   17 GREAT CUMBERLAND PLACE,   LONDON W1A 1AG

Aftim Kreitem,
58 Horncastle Road,
Lee,
London SE12 9EA.   6th April, 1978

Dear Aftim,

RE: F.A. Cup Final

I should like to confirm my earlier arrangement with you
for you to carry out an arabic commentary on the F.A. Cup
Final at Wembley on May 6th.

As previously agreed I.T.C. will pay you the sum of £200
for your services.

As yet I cannot confirm the countries who will be taking
this commentary but will let you know this at a later date.

Yours sincerely,

Peter di Palma

c.c. Mr. R. Weighill
      Mr. B.J. Kingham

AN ⬚ COMPANY

Registered Office: ATV House, 17 Great Cumberland Place, London W1A 1AG. Registered in England No. 609430.

Peter Di Palma

47

At one time I was presenting three programmes in one day: two listener request programmes, one containing Arabic songs and another containing western music and songs, as well as the *Round the Arab World* programme. I also presented and produced a programme called *The World this Morning*, which was a current affairs programme, and *The London Visitor of the Week* programme. I almost became a jack-of-all-trades. As a result my income suddenly increased fourfold. On top of all this, I started to receive invitations from a number of Arab organisations to attend and report on various sporting events. As I was still working freelance, I was free to attend the BBC in fact welcomed these opportunities since it saved them paying for my travel and accommodation. The only expense they incurred was the telephone calls to deliver my reports.

One day, while covering the Gulf Football Cup in Saudi Arabia, a listener learned the name of the hotel where I was staying. He kept contacting me and left so many messages asking to meet me that I promised to meet him at the end of the tournament. When we met, I discovered that he was obsessed with the Arabic Service, to the extent that he knew the name of every one of the station's announcers. When he told me the reason I was astonished. He told me his father had been a general in the Saudi army and one day he had gone to ask him if it was true that in Mecca in 1979 there had been a failed attempt against the governing regime by a jihadist group. The father asked his son where he had heard this news. When the son answered that he had heard it on the radio he had bought, his father demanded that he bring the radio at once, and when he did so, he smashed it to pieces under his feet.

Another surprise came in 1994 after receiving an invitation to attend the Gulf Cooperative Football Championship in Al Ain in the UAE. The invitation came personally from Sheikh Hamdan Ben Mubarak Al-Nahian, whose family owns Manchester City Football Club. The reason for my surprise was that, on finishing an interview with him about the championship, I discovered that not only was he a fan of my work, but he also expressed regret that the monthly cassette *Pick of the Month* had been closed down. This monthly cassette, which was a compilation of all the best reports from the Arabic Service, chosen by me, had been an idea I had taken to the BBC and they had taken up. If I had been left to do the job by myself, the project would have been very cost effective, but, after appointing me as consultant and producer, the BBC had brought in another person, with no experience in the business, to oversee my work. In fact, in order to head up the project, the individual had been transferred from his senior post as the Deputy Head of the Arabic Service and it was due to the high cost of his salary that the venture did not succeed. A month after his arrival, we lost a contract with British Airways, who had been presenting the free cassette to its Middle East travellers. They rejected the following edition because the new boss had opted for a cheaper cassette cover in order to reduce costs, and this cheap cover did not meet the high standards of British Airways. The monthly cassette only lasted for two years. Perhaps the description of the subjects covered in the cassette will give an idea about it.

"HARVEST OF THE MONTH"
"A new monthly talking magazine from the Arabic Service"

"In October 1983 the BBC Arabic Service launched a monthly audio cassette magazine called "HARVEST OF THE MONTH". Each month a specially prepared 60 minute cassette of the most interesting items broadcast by the Arabic Service is compiled and available for sale.

"It is designed to provide our millions of listeners, and many millions of Arabs throughout the world living away from their homeland, with a new way of benefitting from the best of our programmes, giving them an opportunity to build their own special family library of the past and present life of the Arab nation.

"The output from which the selection is made includes programmes about science, technology, medicine, profiles of famous Arab personalities, poems, discussions of the Arabic language and literature, proverbs and their origins, classical and modern music, together with items from our archives which go back 46 years.

"Contents of the 18th edition:

Side 1

1 – Anti-cancer factor: Will it work on humans?
2 – Who killed President Kennedy?
3 – The Empty Quarter
4 – Can't sleep? Take lessons, not pills.
5 – What is the phenomenon of Flying Saucers?
6 – Give a biography of Benito Mussolini.
7 – Diseases of the gums.

Side 2

1 – Why are people mostly right handed?
2 – Season of the Fig in Folklore (continued).
3 – Finger Rings may spread infection in hospitals.
4 – The talk describes the British love of old buildings and poets' haunts.
5 – Focus on the CIA.
6 – Marry a young wife and live longer.
7 – From Saying on a Saying.

Chapter 11
Radical Changes

Radical changes introduced to the External Services late in the nineties resulted in the organisation cancelling most of its cultural and scientific programmes. This radicalization, according to my editor, and later spread round the Service forced Sam Younger, who was the General Director of External Services at the time, to pick up his briefcase and walk out of Bush House, never to return. I knew him very well when he was the Head of the Arabic Service and he regularly used to attend our live broadcasts of the World Cup in 1990. I was the main commentator, sitting alongside various football pundits in front of a TV in a studio in Bush House, far away from Italy. I spent countless hours researching all the teams participating in the tournament and familiarising myself with the photograph and background of every player. The quality of our broadcast was praised by a number of our listeners and certain Egyptian newspapers. Many listeners wrote to tell us how they turned down the sound of their TV and enjoyed our live commentaries on nine matches, including the World Cup Final.

B B C

W O R L D
S E R V I C E

BRITISH BROADCASTING CORPORATION
BUSH HOUSE
PO BOX 76, STRAND
LONDON WC2B 4PH
TELEPHONE: 071 240 3456
TELEX: 265781
CABLES: BROADBRIT LONDON

EXTENSION:
DIRECT LINE:
FAX:

12th July 1990

Aftim Kreitem,
Room 422 NE,
Bush House.

Dear Aftim,

Now that the dust has settled after the World Cup, may I express my appreciation for all your efforts during the live commentaries. From everything I have heard, it seems that the whole operation was very worthwhile and has made a very satisfying impact on the target area. I think you can feel very pleased with some of the comments, especially in the Egyptian press, to the effect that Egyptian commentators mights have something to learn from the way the BBC covered the matches.

Many thanks again.

Yours sincerely,

Sam Younger
Head of the Arabic Service

Copy of Sam Younger letter

Mark Byford, who replaced Sam Younger, accepted the radical changes that were introduced, and later moved on to other departments, eventually becoming Acting Director General of the organisation. According to an article in the *Daily Telegraph* on Wednesday 26 December 2012, he received a redundancy payment of £949,000.

I began to receive invitations from a number of Arab countries, including Syria, Tunis and Oman, to commentate on various sports events. The biggest surprise came when I was invited to report on the Arab Games in Latakia, Syria in 1992. Not for the first time, the invitation included my wife. We were given an official car to take us wherever we needed to go.

On our first visit to the sports stadium, when we disembarked from the car, we were led to the commentary box, where Syria's most famous sports commentator, Adnan Bozo, who is sadly now deceased, was covering the event live. As soon as he saw me, he interrupted his TV broadcast, which was being transmitted via satellite to the whole Arab world, and welcomed me. The words of praise he spoke exceeded anything I could have imagined. Sitting next to him was the Algerian Olympic gold medalist Hasiba Boulmerqa. The next day I found a group of young girls sitting behind the commentary table, waiting for me to sign autographs. They were regular listeners to my *Western Listeners' Request* programme. To find myself in this situation was highly unusual, as it was also for most of my colleagues in Bush House: for normally when we left the building no one ever recognised any of us! That experience, however, proved how popular the Arabic Service was among its targeted audience.

In 1995 another invitation came, this time to cover the African Nations Cup in Tunisia, where again I received generous hospitality from the host country. Despite having to wait until 2 am each morning to file my reports to Bush House and appearing on the country's national TV in a programme alongside prominent personalities, including Dr Havelange, FIFA Director General at the time, I returned to work to find the decision had been taken to deduct from my salary the two weeks' absence in Tunisia, when in reality I had been doing work for the Service. While I suffered this injustice, I personally witnessed a colleague working in the World Service paying $700 for his accommodation in the same hotel in which we had been staying. That injustice was partly corrected when I complained to Benny Ammar, the Head of Region, Africa and Middle East.

My Long Affair with Auntie

B B C

W O R L D
S E R V I C E

BRITISH BROADCASTING CORPORATION
AFRICA & MIDDLE EAST REGION
BUSH HOUSE
PO BOX 76, STRAND
LONDON WC2B 4PH
TELEPHONE: 0171 257 2660
FAX: 0171 240 6227

13th March 1995

Aftim Kreitem
Arabic Service

Dear Aftim,

I am delighted to tell you, that, in recognition of your sustained, outstanding
work, I have decided to award you a bonus of £430.00.

This amount, unfortunately minus the usual deductions, should appear in your
March salary.

Benny Ammar
Head of Region, Africa and Middle East

Copy of the letter from Benny

Chapter 12
Arab Sports Personality
of the Year

To go back to the time when Sam Younger was the Head of the Arabic Service, I seem to have made a good impression on him especially when he used to come to the studio to watch our coverage of the World Cup Finals in 1990. Earlier in his tenure of office he had been the first Head of the Arabic Service to agree to broadcast live football commentary from anywhere other than Wembley stadium. He authorised me to travel to Cairo to present a live broadcast of the World Cup qualifying match between Egypt and Algeria, which resulted in Egypt qualifying for the competition for the first time since 1934. He also takes credit for accepting an idea which I had set my heart on: namely, the staging of the first-ever Arab Sports Personality of the Year. He strongly recommended to his successor Gamon McLellan that this idea should be implemented.

Before Sam Younger's departure, in 1990 I was asked to move from active freelance status to work on a number of contracts, though each contract stipulated (as had been the case in previous years and continued to be in subsequent years) the following clause: "The other provisions of your contract will continue in force, including your agreement that in so far as it is permitted by the current employment legislation, non-renewal of this engagement when its term expires shall not constitute grounds either for a claim of unfair dismissal or for any redundancy payment." The irony of the situation was that this condition neither applied to the person stipulating it nor to the millions of other staff employed by the BBC, including top executives who like me were recruited locally and, after their first year, enjoyed the benefit of joining the pension scheme.

Anyhow, it took me some time to work out how to implement my idea of the Arab Sports Personality of the Year. I started to contact influential sports personalities in the target area starting with Prince Faisal Bin Fahd, the eldest son of King Fahd and President of the Arab Sports Confederation.

Prince Faisal Bin Fahd

Credit must go to him for building the huge sports infrastructure in Saudi Arabia. He warmly welcomed the project, as did many influential sports authorities in various parts of the Arab world. We also started asking our listeners throughout the Arab world to nominate those whom they thought deserved to win the award. The Service was inundated with thousands of letters.

The ceremony and the gala dinner took place at Aida Hall in the Marriott Hotel, Cairo, on 22 November 1992. The nominated athletes attended the ceremony, along with sports ministers from the various Arab states. Although Prince Faisal phoned me at home to apologise that he was unable to attend because of his previously scheduled commitments, he sent Mr Othman Al-Saad, Secretary General of the Arab Games, to represent him at the ceremony, which was broadcast live by the Arabic Service and recorded by Egyptian Television. I went to Cairo airport to receive Mr Al-Saad, and he handed me a large envelope from Prince Faisal addressed to me. When I opened it on reaching my hotel room I was bewildered and astonished because it contained not only a letter in which the Prince expressed admiration of my work but also a gift of $30,000 in cash – a gift so large that it took me a long time to manage to count the notes correctly! Arab generosity is well known and to refuse it would be a great insult. In fact, I appreciated the gift very much as it came from a Prince who dedicated his life to enhancing sport not only in Saudi Arabia but throughout the Arab world. Sadly he died young, aged only 55, His death came immediately after returning home, from attending the Arab Games in Jordan in 1999. On leaving Amman's Airport he promised to donate one million Dollars to an orphanage school in Jordan .His Son prince Nawaf Bin Faisal honoured the pledge .

The following is the letter prince Fahd wrote to me in his own writing

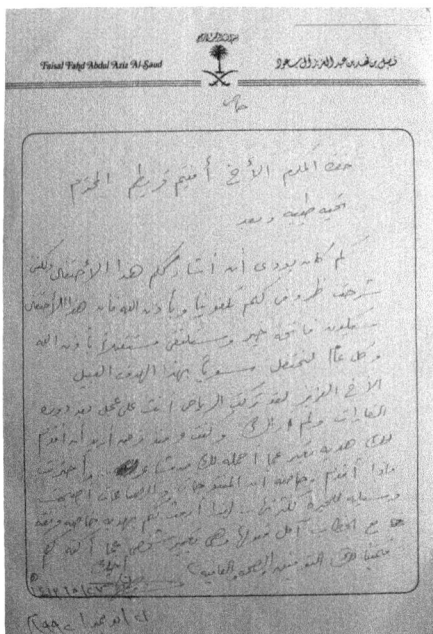

Dear Aftim Kreitem

How much I wanted to attend the ceremony but, as I explained to you over the phone, my protocol-arranged commitments prevent me. God willing, we shall celebrate annually this noble cause.

Dear friend, you left Riyadh in a hurry after attending the Inter-Continental Championship. For a long time I have wanted to present you with a gift to show my appreciation of your work but I was at a loss as to what to present you. Therefore I hope that you will accept my special gift to you which is included in this letter.

His Royal Highness ended his letter by wishing me the best of luck and good health.

The Arab Sports Personality of the Year held in Cairo was praised not only by the sports ministers of the various Arab countries, but also by many Arab newspapers. The male title of Arab Sports Personality of the Year was won by the Algerian 1500-metre,world record holder Noureddine Morcy, while the female title went to the Algerian Hasiba Boulmerka, who was the 1500-metre world champion. Other athletes receiving trophies included the Moroccan Nawal Moutawakel, the winner of the 400-metre hurdles at the Los Angeles Olympics in 1984.

Hona London, the Arabic *Radio Times*, published a report and pictures of the ceremony.

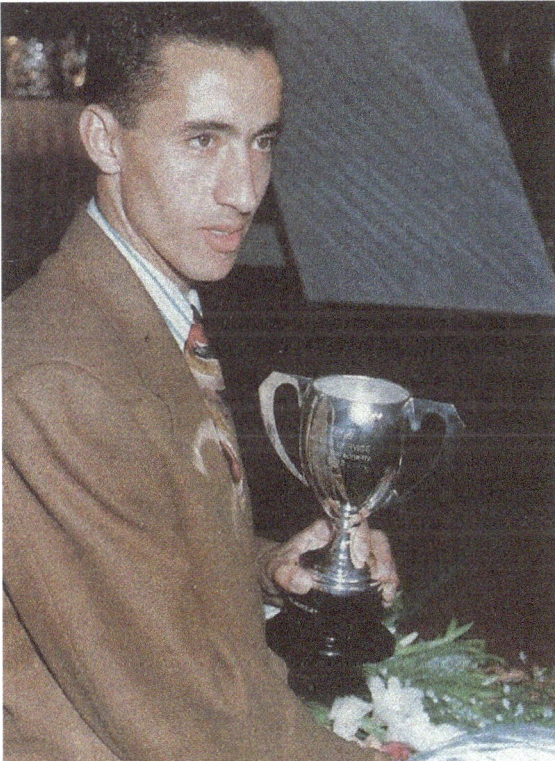

Noureddine Morcy 150 metre World Champion

Author With Hasiba Boulmerka 1500 metre World Champion

Boulmerka and Morcy with their trophies

Great response from our listeners to the first Arab Sports Personality of the Year organised by the BBC Arabic Service.

Al-Maydan, a Jordanian sports magazine, praised the ceremony. Under a column entitled "Only an Opinion", Saleh Asaad wrote:

"Thank you, Radio London (BBC Arabic Service).

We the Arabs have over many years read at school that the English have always pursued a policy to divide us. But this time it is different as the British Broadcasting Corporation, through its Arabic Service and its sports programmes, are working to unite and honour the Arab youth irrespective of their nationalities, and to achieve what the Arab Athletic Federation and the Arab Borough of Sports ministers have failed to achieve. We have seen athletes from Algeria, Morocco, Qatar and Egypt honoured in Cairo during a ceremony attended by Arab sport's ministers and athletes from various Arab states including the Jordanian sports minister Saleh Irshidat. Thanks to the Arabic Service of the BBC for this idea and thanks to its sports programmes and those working on them, particularly Aftim Kreitem, for their efforts and the impartiality they demonstrated, because the result reflected what those heroes have achieved."

On our way back to London there was a discernible change in the attitude of the Head of the Services on our way to Cairo. He insinuated, when I was talking about my programmes, that I am conceited. The change occurred when scores of fans came to the hotel to meet me following the announcement that the ceremony was to be held at the Marriott Hotel. I never showed him copies of Arabic newspapers that wrote about me during my travel in certain parts of the Arab World, which can take a huge part of this book.

Chapter 13
Official Duty Tour

Unlike my colleagues who used to travel regularly, the BBC only sent me on one official trip, and that was in 1980 covering Cairo, Beirut, Damascus and Amman. At that time, because of tension in the area, there was no direct flight to Amman from Beirut airport, so I hired a car to take me to Amman.

When we left the Syrian border, the driver asked me for a favour: he wanted me to allow a student to travel with us to Amman, on the pretext that the Syrians had not allowed him to enter their country to continue his studies there. The student pretended that he had no money to travel back to Jordan. Yet, throughout the whole journey, he never stopped talking against the Jordanian regime, particularly against King Hussein. I disagreed with him, and suspected that he was an informer from the Intelligence Department. My suspicions were confirmed when, the next day, the man with no money came to see me at the Intercontinental hotel and insisted on buying me a drink in the five star establishment!

I returned from the tour laden down with the interviews I had conducted with various officials and famous stars, including Duraid Lahham, who had kindly invited me to his house and later on to a very popular nightclub, where all eyes had been directed towards his table. He is well known for the role he acted as Ghawar Al-Toushe, which made him famous throughout the Arab world.

Some of BBC Arabic Service staff

The most remarkable thing about the BBC Arabic Service is that ladies were allowed to read news bulletins many years before Nan Winton and Angela Ripon became the first women to read news on BBC television. This fact was well illustrated by Mr Al-Issa in his article written for the fiftieth anniversary of the Service in which he praised Madiha Madffai as the best reader of news and poetry. In the same article he credited Rashad Ramadan, the producer of *Listeners' Forum*, with being the receiver of the most mail in Bush House. I was also included in his article: "Football fans from the Arab world gather in their clubs to listen to Aftim Kreitem, from Wembley Stadium." And he went on to say: "A son of my friend in Geneva phoned me to see if I could arrange for him to meet Aftim Kreitem. A few days after the conversation, he appeared in Bush House, and I took him to meet Aftim. After leaving his office he said, 'Now I can go back to Geneva feeling proud that I have met Aftim.'"

The Service's fiftieth anniversary was an opportunity to dig into the archives to publish pictures of the various kings, presidents and famous personalities who had appeared before the BBC microphones, such as King Hassan the Second of Morocco being interviewed by Hassan Al-Karmi, the most famous broadcaster in the Arabic Service. He had achieved his fame through his literature and poetry programme *Saying on Saying*. Despite the many years he spent in the Arabic Service and despite being a first-class broadcaster, the highest position he reached was head of a unit. It was not until the year 2000 that an Arab held the key position of Head of the Service for the first time, and he only held the post for a short period. Also no Arab employee was allowed to edit the news, write current affairs talks or answer a political question. On one occasion, when the producer of a political question and answer programme did answer a question about the attitude of the British government towards Palestine, he was reprimanded, evoking a strong protest from the majority of the staff, and he never did so again. That job was entrusted only to British experts.

Chapter 14
The Crucial Difference

While the whole of BBC radio and television are technically part of the same organisation and controlled by the same management and governance boards, until recently not all its departments received a share of the licence revenue. The External Services used to receive a direct grant from the Foreign Office.

The success of the BBC Home Service and television relied on two important factors: content and talent. Unfortunately, within the Arabic Service the latter was not always reflected in the financial remuneration received by its talented staff. As a good example the annual earnings of some broadcasters within the Home Services was so inflated that some could earn in the seventies over £100,000 annually, which was a good incentive for them to opt out of their pensionable posts in favour of engagement by contract, enabling them to afford their own generous private pensions. Within the Arabic Service itself priority for pensionable posts was given to translators rather than talented broadcasters, with the only person authorised to transfer a programme assistant to a pensionable post being the Head of the Service.

At my time in the sixties and seventies broadcasters used to be selected to read the news. Discrimination within the Arabic Service was not unknown. Many new recruits who joined more than ten years after me were transferred to pensionable posts, before being able to build a name for their career.

One day I sat to have lunch in the BBC canteen with J.A.F. Morton, who shot up from Senior Personnel Officer in the Arabic Service to a very senior post within the organisation. Being aware of my situation from his previous work in the Arabic Service, he told me frankly that if I took a discrimination case to court I would win. The courage he showed in making this statement was unbelievable, I wonder what his attitude would have been to learn that I left the BBC, after almost thirty-seven years, without even having a cup of coffee with the Head of Service, to thank me for my long service. My wife and I did not want to take a discrimination case to court. When I told three professional friends from outside the organisation about the treatment I received, they each separately came out with one word: "disgraceful". Equally shocked was the sports editor of the Jordanian newspaper *Al-Raay* when I went to see him in his office to thank him for the column he had written about me: he could not believe that I had left the BBC without a pension and not even a cup of coffee.

In spite of the setbacks, I resumed my dedicated service. I was now focusing a great deal of attention on how best to organise the next Arab Sports Personality of the Year, with a view to broadcasting the ceremony not only on radio but also on television. The Head of the Arabic Service asked my advice on how best to pursue influential sports people in the Arab world, to support the event. I suggested the ceremony should be held in Doha, the capital of Qatar. My contact there was Mr Ali Al-Fardan, one of the wealthiest men in the Gulf, who happened to be the President of Qatar Tennis and Squash Federation.

The first time I met Mr Al-Fardan had been in London in June 1992, when he came to publicise the first ATP tennis tournament, which was due to be held in his country from 4th–10th January 1993. He seemed to have been impressed by articles I had written on tennis history and various tennis tournaments, especially the Grand Slams, and in Arab publications including our own sports magazine. When I learned of his initiative in staging the tennis ATP tournament in Qatar, I invited him to Bush House to tell me about it. I responded enthusiastically and offered my assistance in promoting it internationally. We met several times in a well-known Lebanese restaurant in London, together with my journalist friend Peter Jolly, who was the Editor in Chief of the Kentish Times: which used to sponsor the Beckenham Tournament before the Wimbledon Tennis Championship and offered his advice on how to extend invitations to British tennis journalists to help opening an international press office in Qatar.

After leaving the restaurant I continued my work on how to stage the second Arab Sport Personality of the Year, with the possibility not only to broadcast the event live on radio but also on television.

I wrote a letter to Prince Faisal, President of the Arab Sports Confederation, asking him to support the initiative. He replied not only giving his support for what he called this "noble idea", but also inviting me and the Head of the Arabic Service to visit him in Riyadh. Despite restrictions on British journalists entering Saudi Arabia at the time, he asked the Saudi embassy in London to issue the required visas. The Head was pleased with the Prince's response.

Chapter 15
The VIP Experience

Not long after that, the BBC bought two economy tickets for us to fly to Riyadh. I remember that on the same flight was the new British ambassador, who was going out to present his credential papers. Gamon McLellan, the Head of the Arabic Service at the time, went more than once to talk to him in the first class compartment. When the plane landed at Riyadh International Airport at 4.30 am, an announcement came over loud speakers asking Mr Kreitem to introduce himself. I walked, along with Gamon McLellan, towards the front of the plane and as soon as the door opened, we encountered a number of cameramen and journalists who had gathered on the tarmac, before being led through the VIP area to where Dr Nasser, the deputy of Prince Faisal, was waiting to welcome us. The ambassador to be and his companions were following behind us, while all the cameras were directed at us. The ambassador was heard to say to the Head of the Arabic Service, "Hey, Gamon, all the press attention is on you!" Dr Nasser responded immediately by saying that Mr Kreitem and Mr McLellan are special guests of his Royal Highness Prince Faisal Bin Fahd. Mr McLellan was astonished by the level of the reception we received.

The next day we went to meet Prince Faisal at his office, where his brother Prince Sultan was also present. After expressing our thanks for the invitation, we began to discuss how the Prince could assist us in our efforts to stage the Arab Sports Personality of the Year not in Riyadh but in Doha, the capital of Qatar. He started by saying how pleased he was, "to welcome this noble idea, and willing to assist in whatever Mr Kreitem suggested." I said first that we would like him to attend the ceremony to present the trophy to the winner. He accepted with pleasure, and then continued by expressing his willingness to buy air tickets for the forty-two candidates for the various awards to enable them to travel from any part of the Arab world to Qatar and back to their countries.

At the Prince's Office

When we arrived back, the Head wrote a letter to Sam Younger, the Director General of External Services, to say that the visit had been very successful to the extent that if we had asked for one million pounds we would have got it.

To build on this success, the Head asked if I knew any influential sports person in Qatar. In response I told him about Mr Ali Al-Fardan, the President of the Squash and Tennis Federation in Qatar, who I knew was planning to come to

London in ten days' time. I had already assured my colleagues of his willingness to help in our project to stage the Arab Sports Personality in his country. His respect for me was evident since one day he had delayed the start of a press conference he had called in London for half an hour because I was late in arriving due to traffic. On that occasion he had with him the President of the ATP, in order to announce that his country was to stage its first-ever women's tennis tournament. In the meantime the Head authorised the spending of £1200 on various trophies, and we began to publicise the event, asking our listeners to nominate their favourite athletes.

Ten days later Mr Al-Fardan arrived in London – he was staying at the Lanesborough Hotel in central London. The Head of Arabic Service asked Hani Al-Arabi, the editor of the unit in which I worked, and Kevin Whitingham, the editor of *Hona London* magazine, to go with us to the meeting. After introducing them to Ali Al-Fardan, the Head began to explain the plan. I was surprised at Mr Al-Fardan's response since it was exactly the same as Prince Faisal's had been. He welcomed the "noble idea" and said he would support whatever Mr Kreitem suggested. I proposed that the ideal place to stage the ceremony would be the Sheraton Hotel in Doha, based on my experience of staying there with my wife as his guests and also of all the tennis stars who had stayed there during the First Qatar Open. Mr Al-Fardan volunteered to pay the expenses of the gala dinner at the hotel, as long as the Arabic Service met the accommodation costs of the athletes staying at the hotel for two nights, and he also volunteered to pay any other expenses regarding the transmission of the event by satellite. All this pleased the Head. Mr Al-Fardan covered the cost of hosting us in the five star hotel.

Mr. Al-Fardan and Boris Becker

The next day when I arrived at Bush House, I noticed that the Head and Kevin Whitingham were having a meeting in the office of Hani Al-Arabi, and the latter signalled to me to enter his office. He told me bluntly that they had decided that he and Kevin – who had nothing whatsoever to do with sport – were to travel without me to Qatar to finalise the arrangements for the ceremony. I could smell a rat – not for the first time during my long service at the BBC! And my hunch proved right. I felt completely confident through my good contacts that the Arabic Service could not do the ceremony without me. How furious I felt became abundantly clear to them when I said: "After all my hard work you want to throw me out of my own idea!" The editor responded by saying, "How dare you talk to us like that!" and I walked out. It is said that an ambitious person always feels the injustice more than anything else.

After taking a few days to think about what response I should make based on my previous experience, I phoned Mr Al-Fardan, who by now had returned to his country. I explained the situation to him, telling him that they wanted to cut me out of my own idea. He said, "Don't worry, Aftim. Let them come and I shall not meet them." He honoured his pledge, and they returned to London without seeing him.

Even when later, a more senior BBC official travelled to Doha, he returned with the same result. A great proof of the end of the golden age of the Arabic Service came when the ceremony was cancelled without even an apology to the listeners. One can imagine what sort of publicity the Arabic Service would have gained if the project had been allowed to continue, following the huge success of our first ceremony held in Cairo on Sunday 22 November 1992.

Chapter 16
The Television Experience

Despite the huge setback of the abandonment of the Arab Sports Personality of the Year, not for the first time in my career I resumed my job without any hesitation. I continued to produce and present various programmes with boundless energy and dedication, doing shift work and writing about sport in *Hona London* magazine and other Arabic publications.

It was my long experience in broadcasting that helped me to overcome the most difficult situation I ever had to face in my broadcasting career! It occurred one day when the time came for me to read live the five-minute sports news slot, which I used to translate from English to Arabic in my own handwriting. I used to write the running order in English and under it write the Arabic script. However, when I reached the studio I found that under the running order there were a number of sheets of blank paper and the sports news was missing. I ran back to my office to fetch my script, but I could not find it. So I rushed back to the studio, switched on the microphone and started to deliver the sports news from memory based on the news which I had already translated and, thanks to the good experience I had gained from broadcasting the FA Cup Final live, I managed to avoid what could have been a very embarrassing situation. In fact, the continuity announcer did not even notice that anything was wrong. But the biggest surprise came when I returned to my office and found that the sports news bulletin had unintentionally been put in the bin.

As the first APT Tennis Tournament in Qatar was approaching I wrote about tennis, explaining the rules of tennis in simple terms so that anybody could follow the game. In fact, when I arrived in Doha, the Qatar TV Channel asked me to make a programme about tennis and its rules. Two cameramen joined me at a tennis court, along with Nasser Al-Khelaifi who, as a Qatari, got a wild card to the tournament. With him standing opposite me on the tennis court, I started to talk to the camera without a script about the rules of the game and how the points are counted. As the ball was moving between us, my explanation was clear and simple. At the time Nasser was sixteen years old and now is the Chief Executive of Paris Saint German Football Club and President of Qatar Tennis Federation. The programme had a good response despite it being my first attempt at TV.

My wife and I went to Qatar as the special guests of Mr Al-Fardan. In addition to introducing the opening and closing ceremonies of the tournament, I also travelled backwards and forwards to the airport to welcome the tennis stars, which gave me the opportunity to conduct interviews with them for the Arabic Service. My only disappointment was that the tournament was not covered live in Arabic on TV, although I had expressed to Mr Al-Fardan my willingness to do the commentary. But the object of the tournament, as I learnt later, was to cover it worldwide in English in order to show to the world the progress Qatar had achieved in a short number of years. But the late John Parsons, tennis correspondent of the *Daily Telegraph*, told me that he thought the tournament would have made a greater impact if a Qatari had won the title. I personally believe that if we had covered it in Arabic, we could have had more success in popularising tennis in the Arab world. The Al-Jazeera Channel did not exist at the time. All this was done out of my love for the game and in my capacity as an active freelancer with the BBC. Also my work was entirely free, apart from the free air travel and accommodation provided at the Sheraton Hotel, which I had thought could be an ideal venue for the ceremony of the second Arab Sports Personality of the Year.

بســــــــم الله الرّحمن الرّحيــــــم

State of Qatar
Qatar Tennis & Squash Federation

دَوْلَــة قطَــر
الإتحاد القَطَريّ للتنس والإسكواش

No: QTSF/603

الـرقم :

Date: 22/07/1992

التاريخ :

To :   Mr. Aftim E. Kreitem - TV Sport Commentator

From : Mr. Ali Al - Fardan

Subject : Qatar Open 4-10 January 1993

Dear Mr. Kreitem,

I enjoyed meeting you during wimbledon and all the discussion about our tournament, also I would like to thank you for your help and co-operation during this period to introduce your ideas for our event.

So it gives me great pleasure to invite you as a special guest for our Qatar Open 4-10 January 1993.

Qatar Tennis and Squash Federation will be responsible for all costs relating to the above subject the traveling tickets and full accommodation.

Please confirm your acceptance of our invitation to allow us making the necessary arrangements.

Hoping to see you soon in Doha.

Best regards,

Ali Al - Fardan
President

صندوق بريد ٤٩٥٩ الدوحة ـ قطر . هاتف ٣٥١١٣١ . ٣٥١١٢٩ . فاكس ٣٥١٦٣١ . تلكس ٤٧٤٩
P.O. Box - 4959 — Doha - Qatar — Tel : 351631 - 351629 — Fax : 351631 — Tlx.: 4749 QAT FOT DH

Mr. Al-Fardan invitation

The only time I was unable to do the commentary for the FA Cup Final was on 20 May 1989, the day my son and his wife-to-be chose to get married. That was the only day in over forty years that the Arabic Service failed to broadcast the FA Cup Final live professionally, because the person who replaced me did not find the job as easy as he thought he would, commenting later to colleagues that he had assumed he only needed to know the names of the players! It was sad that none of my colleagues were able to provide an adequate commentary in my absence. It was a great match between Liverpool and Everton, with Liverpool winning 3-2 after extra time. After that I resumed doing the regular live commentaries in addition to my usual work. But, most unfortunately, in 1993 the Service took the drastic decision to cease broadcasting the live football commentaries which after over three decades had become a remarkable annual tradition. Protests came from many listeners, including from a prominent guest, Mr Mansour Al-Khodairy of the Arab Sports Federation.

Chapter 17
The Al-Jazeera TV Experience

In the years that followed I attended two Gulf Cup of Nations football competitions, one in Abu Dhabi in 1994 and the other in Oman in 1996. While I was in Oman I met Ayman Jada, a football stringer for the Arabic Service, who invited me to meet with him because he wanted to tell me about the forthcoming launch of the Al-Jazeera Channel in Qatar. He told me that he was going to be appointed as the Head of the Sports Channel and asked me if I would work with him in his unit. I welcomed the offer as long as I could remain in London. So when Al-Jazeera's main channel launched in 1996 I started to contribute regularly, while still continuing to work with the BBC as a freelancer.

Meanwhile at the BBC, following the failure of my idea of hosting the second Arab Sports Personality of the Year, from 1993 onwards deliberate obstacles began to be put in my way and this continued until my final departure in September 2000. The first time it happened was when I received two invitations: one from Prince Faisal to attend the Continental Football Championship in Riyadh and the other from Mr Al-Fardan to attend the third ATP tournament in Doha. On both occasions, despite me pleading with the editor to allow me to cover these two very important sports events, I was refused permission to travel since at this time I was on a short-term contract . As a result I submitted my resignation, but to my surprise I was asked to withdraw it. In the end we reached the compromise that I would continue my work on a freelance basis. Nevertheless, I, and maybe the Service too, missed covering the two events.

Meanwhile the Olympic Games in Sydney was approaching and I expressed my great interest to cover it for the Service. In the letter I sent to the Head of the Service on 12 January 2000 – which was almost 8 months before the event:

"As a result of the wind of change currently blowing over the Service, there is no better news than covering the Sydney Olympics from 13 September to first of October 2000. I am writing to renew my enthusiasm and confirm my availability and sincere wish to represent the Service in Sydney. I am doing so despite my previous failed attempts to represent the Service in major sporting events, including the 1998 Football World Cup.

For a professional and dedicated Sport Broadcaster/ Commentator, there is no better cherished dream to realise during his or her career than covering the Olympics once in a lifetime.

This is my final attempt which is not based on emotional grounds but based on reality that no other colleague has and presented the Sports Magazine more than myself in the history of the Arabic Service. You personally were kind to me when you wrote to say: "You generally do an excellent job of representing the BBC in dealings with figures in the Arab World involved with Sport" (dated 27 May 1993).

During my long career with the BBC, I have collected similar acclaims from various listeners, Arab newspapers, magazines, and TV programmes, which are not practical to include. Sorry to blow my own trumpet, however this is for no other reason than to support how much the Service can benefit, not only from the great gathering of sports personalities, but also from my dedication to make our presence a great success.

For this, I repeat the package that I have already offered the former editor Aref Hijjawi, to produce and present live from Sydney a daily Olympic programme up to 20 minutes duration, at a cost effective of £160 per programme, plus usual BBC travel and expenses.

I am willing to take this challenge despite the very hard work it entails."

The last straw that broke the camel's back came a few months before the start of the Olympic Games in Sydney, when the Service decided to send a colleague who had no experience in sports coverage to cover the big event. I wrote to the Head complaining, but for two whole months he refrained from answering my letter, until I confronted him outside his office and demanded a response. When he did eventually answer the letter, he wrote to say that the decision had already been taken and he could not change it.

British Broadcasting Corporation Bush House PO Box 76 Strand London WC2B 4PH Telephone 0171 240 3456

B B C World Service

DIRECT NO. (00)44 207 557 2534
FAX: (00) 44 207 379 1588
E-MAIL: Gamon.McLellan@bbc.co.uk
08 February 2000

Mr. Aftim E. Kreitem
Arabic Service

Dear Aftim,

Thank you for your memo of 12 January, and I apologise for not having replied earlier.

I fully appreciate your interest in covering the Olympics for us from Sydney, and it was good of you to put forward the proposal. However, earlier this year we took a decision to nominate Amr Al-Kahky to go to Sydney and cover this for us. This is certainly not a criticism of the work you have done in putting sport on the map for the Arabic Service. I am sure you would have done an excellent job, and I would like to re-emphasise our appreciation of all you have done in the sports area for the Arabic Service. I hope you will not be too disappointed by this decision.

Best wishes,
Yours ever,

Gamon McLellan

Copy of the kind letter

Despite these generous words I did not change my mind about what is right and what is wrong, and so I told him sadly that September 15 would be my last day working in the Arabic Service, which would be on the eve of the Olympic Games in Sydney; that evening was indeed the last day I worked at the BBC after nearly thirty-seven years.

Sadly the BBC, the great media organisation and number one in the world, is not immune to infallibility by individual mistakes, such as a member of staff who received a letter from the Director General of the BBC expressing regret over his resignation, not knowing that he took one year sick leave in order to expand his private business. In contrast to that, a person who dedicated over 37 years loyal service did not receive a farewell drink. Although I shall treasure the many letters of appreciation:

From: Head of Arabic Service

Room No. &
Building   434 CB BUSH   Tel.
                                        Ext. 2534   date 30th March 1988

Subject: DUTY TOUR

To: Afteim Kreitem   cc: Organiser, Features & Music

many thanks for your excellent report on what was a very productive trip. Your comment on the obvious popularity of sport in the Arab World confirms the need to expand our sports coverage.

I would also like to place on record my appreciation of your coverage of the opening of the new stadium in Riyadh and the Gulf football championship.

On the financial side, it would simplify things if you signed contracts for your despatches, and for the interviews to the total amount agreed with A.H.A.S.

[signature]

[R. Jobbins]

Cat. No. 6912
AS/20

Bob Jobbins former Head of The Arabic Service.

B B C

BRITISH BROADCASTING CORPORATION

PO BOX 76 BUSH HOUSE STRAND LONDON WC2B 4PH

TELEPHONE 01·240 3456 TELEX· 265781

TELEGRAMS AND CABLES: BROADBRIT LONDON TELEX

20th November 1975

Mr. A. Kreitem,
Rm. 407

Dear Aftim,

    I would like to record my appreciation
of the excellent work you did during the
Dawn Transmission today. It is the spontaneous
and correct reaction on such occasions that
enables the BBC Arabic Service to maintain
its lead over all competitors.

    I am sending a copy of this note to
H. Arabic S.

           Yours sincerely,

           Christopher Child

Copy to H. Arabic S.

Christopher Child former Programme Organiser.

B B C

BRITISH BROADCASTING CORPORATION

PO BOX 76 BUSH HOUSE STRAND LONDON WC2B 4PH

Ext. 2540

TELEPHONE 01-240 3456 TELEX: 265781

TELEGRAMS AND CABLES: BROADBRIT LONDON TELEX

20th November 1975

Dear Aftim,

Thank you very much indeed for handling the announcement of the death of General Franco and the consequential
programme changes with such professional skill. You have
my warmest congratulations.

I am glad we had our conversation on the telephone
which was extremely useful.

I returned to bed and slept soundly for an hour and
a half knowing that the transmission was in safe hands.

Kindest regards,

Yours sincerely,

Ronald H. Icke

A. Kreitem, Esq.,
Room 407,
CB Bush.

Ronald Icke former Head News and Presentations.

BBC

BRITISH BROADCASTING CORPORATION
TELEVISION CENTRE
WOOD LANE
LONDON W12 7RJ
TELEPHONE: 0181 743 8000
FAX: 0181 749 7435

16 May, 1996

Mr Eftim Kreitem
76 Meadow Court Road
Black Heath
London SE3 9DY

Dear Eftim

As you will probably know, BBC Arabic Television ceased production as of 21 April 1996. I should like to take this opportunity to thank you for your contribution to the success of the channel during its lifetime. It was contributions such as yours that really enhanced the programmes, and helped make the channel unique by providing accurate and fair television coverage of news and current affairs in Arabic to the Arab world.

Thank you again for every thing you did to help us make the BBC Arabic Television the success it was.

Yours sincerely,

enjoy Euro 96

Charles Richards
Editor, Arabic Television

Charles Richards Former Head of BBC Arabic Television.

But one of the secret powers of Auntie is that whenever I travelled by air to the Middle East, I was upgraded to first class or business.

In the meantime, the well-known sports company TWI put my name forward to be the main commentator for the Lebanon Broadcasting Company (LBC) for the 1994 Wimbledon Tennis Championships. This recommendation came as a result of my work in covering the ATP tournament in Qatar, which TWI was also covering. This was a great opportunity for me to comment on tennis, which I cherished, having played the game myself for many years and done a great deal of work to find the correct Arabic translation for all aspects of the game including the tie break introduced in 1970, which I translated into Arabic as *almahsama* translation, I later saw recognised in one Arabic dictionary, but it is sadly no longer used in the press or on radio. Sadly also, the subtle difference between a seed and rank and many other technical tennis terms are yet to be recognised. The LBC TV station sent a female commentator to London to work with me on covering Wimbledon. She used the Lebanese dialect while I used the classical Arabic that was practiced in the BBC Arabic Service. We worked together from 12.00 noon to 10 pm, without a break, with me doing the last hour of highlights from the day's play by myself. At the end I was delighted to hear that the producer in Beirut was extremely pleased with our work.

For the next two years the Art Satellite TV station covered the event for most of the Arab world. This time I was assisted by the Algerian tennis coach Jamal Djamel, who was based in Monaco. Credit goes to my wife who assisted me by providing me with the number of aces and other statistics from the monitors of other commentators. The following year we had our own monitor for statistics at extra cost. The big difference between the Arabic coverage and that of the BBC is that the latter has a whole team of commentators. Despite the hard and professional work we put in, the only appreciation we received came from a number of the presidents of Arab Tennis Federations. TWA was pleased with my work and offered me a contract with a salary that was 25% less than my current annual income including my BBC income. I declined. On hindsight it was a mistake as TWI has grown to become a huge organisation with a significant presence in worldwide sport.

My freelance work with Al-Jazeera included interviewing players and managers in the football Premier League. I also visited many football premier clubs and reported on their histories, and interviewed famous players, and covered press conferences. When Al-Jazeera Sports Channel started in 2002 my work expanded, and we produced two one-hour documentary programmes, one on Manchester United Football Club, and another on Fulham Football Club when it was owned by Mohamed Al-Fayed. These programmes were very much appreciated by the Head of Al-Jazeera Channel and by viewers. While we were filming outside Old Trafford Stadium, I instructed the crew that if anybody asked about which channel we were filming for, they were to say it was for an overseas station. When I tried to speak to a person entering the club through the executive gate, he refused to talk to me until I identified the channel I was working for. I replied that he would not recognise the channel, as it was then only two years old. On his insistence I said: Al-Jazeera Channel. He immediately said, "Bin Laden." That wrong impression was completely unjustified, as I would never have compromised my long broadcasting career by working with an unprofessional station. Nowadays, most people, having watched its English channel, now know the truth about Al-Jazeera's good name. But sadly, on another occasion, when we were filming the annual county tennis championship in Eastbourne, a British journalist approached my cameraman and asked him the name of the channel filming the event, so he replied, "Al-Jazeera." The next day a well-known newspaper published a very sarcastic piece written by this reporter about our presence at the tournament. He did not know that our intention in filming there was to show our audience in the Arab world the small margin of difference between the standard achieved by the county players as compared with the professional players. The aim of our report was very much to communicate the high standard of play amongst the British county players.

The Al-Jazeera Sports Channel started transmission early in 2002. It broadcast live commentaries on football matches, including the Spanish and English Leagues, and the FA Cup, from the third round up to the final. It provided the right opportunity for me to renew my involvement in this most famous competition worldwide. Working for Al-Jazeera I presented live coverage of every FA Cup Final that was held at the Millennium Stadium in Cardiff during the rebuilding of the Wembley Stadium as well as the first final played at the new Wembley Stadium in 2007. My job also included interviewing players after matches. Up until the new millennium I managed to interview football managers and players face to face for the main Al-Jazeera Channel, but then, as a result of the increase in the number of international channels, it became more difficult. A good example of the change that occurred is illustrated by the response I received when I asked Chelsea Football Club for an interview with Gianfranco Zola before the FA Cup Final against Aston Villa in 2000. I was surprised to learn from the club that the cost of interviewing him would be £10,000 – but free during a press conference. I opted to interview him free during a press conference.

Chapter 18
Sharq Al-Adna Radio Station

Mahatato Al-Sharq Al-Adna Lilithaat Alarabia (the full name in Arabic), or in English the Near East Arab Broadcasting Station (NEABS), was established in Palestine in 1941 by the British. It was based first in Jenin, a small town at that time, with a population of less than 10,000. The reason it was placed there was because it was near the British Army Headquarters. The station offered a wide range of programmes, including drama, poetry, entertainment and music. I have already spoken of its staggering rise from humble origins to the pinnacle of radio stations in the Middle East, with the name of the station growing in the estimation of its listeners until it achieved almost Hollywood status in the Arab world. This remarkable success can be attributed in part to the way the station was run and its ability to create the impression in its listeners that it was more or less an Arab station.

According to the best veteran broadcasters at the time, Kamel Costandi, Sobhi Abo Loghd, Abdulmajid AboLaban, Sabri Al-Sharif and Ghanem Al-Dajani, in interviews given to the Lebanese magazine *Arab Resource Centre for Popular Arts* (December 1996), British staff at the station sympathised with their Palestinian colleagues to such an extent that they closed their eyes to the smuggling of armaments to Palestinian rebels using vehicles owned by the station. This fact contradicted what was later revealed regarding who was running the station and from where the money came to finance it.

At the end of the British Mandate in Palestine in 1948 Sharq Al-Adna was moved to Limassol in Cyprus, which at the time was a British colony. In addition it had studios in Beirut and Cairo, and its own correspondents in these and other Arab countries, who sent news reports back to the main studios in Limassol. The station also had its own orchestra. Despite its big name and fame throughout the Arab world, its studios in Polimidia near Limassol were actually a collection of huts, with medium-wave and short-wave transmitters directed towards the Arab world. Its Arab staff numbered around 150, according to Richard Beeston, one of the editors of NEABS, and in addition there were a few British editors and administrators.

The main purpose of the few commentaries written by the British staff was to seek to communicate to Arab listeners the wisdom of the British Middle East policy, with a pro-Arab, anti-communist slant. The veteran Arab broadcasters, as well as the rest of the station staff, thought that the British Foreign Office was happy to finance the station in order to protect British interests in the MiddleEast. The cordial relations between all staff including the Head and the way the station was run were remarkably successful in creating the impression among the listeners that it was more or less an Arab station. The best Arab artists and writers contributed to its programmes. Even the top Egyptian musician Mohammad Abdulwahab gave Sharq Al-Adna exclusive rights to one of his popular songs, "Al-Nahro Al-Khaled" ("The Eternal River"). The station published a glossy brochure offering potential advertisers the chance to reach markets throughout the Middle East, a service which it boasted no other radio in the area could rival.

The staff enjoyed both their work and the facilities provided for them, which included being transported by the station buses to picnics at various landmark places on the island, and by private boat to beautiful beaches, in addition to an annual banquet hosted by the director. Documents revealing more of the history of the station (and also the Suez Crisis) can be found at the BBC Written Archive Centre in Caversham.

No one could have anticipated that the Suez Crisis would bury this famous radio station and lead to the fall of the British government under Sir Anthony Eden.In fact, the bones of the NEABS staff who have since departed this world would turn in their graves at the revelation, almost forty years after its closure, that the station was operated by MI6. From my experience in Sharq Al-Adna, working as a studio manager, albeit for no more than three years, I like most of my colleagues admired President Nasser of Egypt, especially during his broadcasts on pan-Arab nationalism.

In mid-October 1956 an unusual notice appeared on the station noticeboard, announcing a general staff meeting, but a few hours later it was withdrawn, only to reappear two weeks later. The reason the meeting was initially called turned out to be a false alarm, since an Israeli force had attacked an Arab village near Hebron on the West Bank, but on the second occasion the concern was very real as Israeli forces were advancing towards the Suez Canal.

The meeting took place at Sharq Al-Adna's club in the centre of Limassol on 30 October 1956, and was chaired by Ralph Poston, the director of the station. He asked us to switch on the radio in the hall of the club and listen to an announcement read by a senior colleague. It was, in fact, an ultimatum by Britain and France, who were threatening to use force to separate the Egyptian and the Israeli troops in order to protect the Suez Canal. The staff were shocked to learn from Mr Poston that from now on until further notice the station would be known as Voice of Britain, and the station's transmitters would be used to carry the official announcements of Her Majesty's Government in the UK, and the same transmitters would also be used by the BBC Arabic Service. In order to calm the feelings of the staff Mr Poston agreed to broadcast the following statement after the meeting: "As director of Sharq Al-Adna station, I wish it to be known that the Arab staff of this station are obliged under the circumstances existing in Cyprus to remain at work. Listeners must understand that the feelings of the staff are naturally with their Arab brothers, and they are no longer free agents."

This broadcast was picked up by the BBC Caversham listening post, and Mr Poston and his wife were immediately put under house arrest. When the Arab staff heard that their director had been treated in this fashion, the response was to walk out en masse.

(In my possession I have more than 200 editions of the Sharq Al-Adna bi-monthly magazine, left to me by my late brother Michael, who carefully preserved them. As well as containing articles by the most famous Arab authors and writers of the time, they also include a series of nine articles written by Mr Poston, recounting his memories of a period of time he spent in Moscow during 1947, where he worked as a press attaché in the British Embassy, before being appointed general manager of NEABS.

As some Arab young men were inclined to support the Soviet Union, Mr Poston wrote about the impressions he had gained while living in Moscow. He spoke about the difficulty foreigners faced when they came to look for accommodation, as it was not in their hands, but in the hands of a special committee, who arranged places for them to live where the secret police could keep their eye on them. Embassies were also placed in one building. Foreigners were not allowed to employ maids unless they were registered at the Foreign Office, and people were very aware that their maids, guards and drivers were informers.

To join the communist party was not an easy task, and many of those who applied were refused. Mr Poston went on to talk about what advantages people gained when joining the communist party, as members could avoid long supermarket queues and could avoid travelling on public transport which was very crowded.

Mr Poston had been shocked to learn from one listener in Iraq that he did not believe what he had written in the bi-monthly NEABS magazine.)

When they left the meeting at the club, all the staff were in a state of shock and were convinced without a shadow of a doubt that the Suez War was a result of a tripartite aggression and collusion between Britain, France and Israel. This fact was confirmed thirty years later when the official papers were released.

A short time after returning to England with his wife, Ralph Poston became a vicar, before converting to Islam. He ended his life in a nursing home.

The answer to the mystery surrounding Sharq Al-Adna was revealed by a BBC Radio 4 programme on 15 September 1994, almost thirty-eight years after its closure, with the help of documents disclosed under Whitehall's open government initiative. Up until that time the British government, whenever asked in the House of Commons about the matter, had denied any association. But at the BBC Written Archive Centre in Caversham, near Reading, documents had been found relating to the Suez Crisis which also appeared to make reference to the ownership and financing of Sharq Al-Adna. In 1948 there had been an exchange in the House of Commons during which a left-wing MP, a certain Mr Pirrattin, had questioned Mr Bevin, at that time Foreign Secretary, on the ownership of the station. In reply Mr Bevin had stated that it was operated by a body of people connected with the Arabs. That was not a truthful reply. The Radio 4 programme *Suez: The Propagation of Truth*, produced by Nigel Acheson, unearthed a crucial BBC memo, marked confidential, from the controller of the BBC World Service to his boss, the Director of External Services, dated just before the Suez Crisis, which contained the following key sentence: "Sharq Al-Adna on the technical side will continue to act as the agent of Her Majesty's government."

The Suez Invasion was sparked off by a speech President Gamal Abdul Nasser of Egypt made on 26 July 1956, in which he announced the nationalisation of the Suez Canal Company, following his failure to get a loan from the West to build the Aswan Dam. Revenue from the canal would, he said, be used to finance the dam project. The British government, increasingly aware of the need to counter anti-British propaganda, carried on broadcasting via the Voice of Arabs from Cairo. In a secret meeting in late October 1956, in Sèvres near Paris, representatives of France, Britain and Israel colluded in hatching a plot against Egypt, agreeing to take the following steps:

1. On the evening of 29 October 1956 the Israeli forces would launch a large-scale attack on Egyptian forces, with the aim of reaching the Canal Zone the following day.

2. On being appraised of this situation, the following day the British and French governments would respectively, and simultaneously, make two appeals to the Egyptian government, and the Israeli government along the following lines:

   A. To the Egyptian government:
      a. halt all acts of war;
      b. withdraw all troops ten miles from the Canal;
      c. accept temporary occupation of key positions on the Canal by the Anglo-French forces to guarantee freedom of passage through the Canal by vessels of all nations until final settlement.

   B. To the Israeli government:
      a. halt all acts of war;
      b. withdraw all troops ten miles from the Canal.

But worse propaganda to come was emanating from the new station: "This is the Voice of Britain calling Egyptian sailors, soldiers and airmen. Now listen carefully to this, you are hidden in small villages, do you know what this means? It means your wives, children, mothers, fathers and grandfathers, escaping their houses, and leaving behind their property behind, we will find and bomb you wherever you are."

This British broadcast was carried on the same wavelength as programmes from the BBC Arabic Service, and as a result the Arabic Service came under strong political pressure during the Suez Crisis. The BBC was justly proud of the way it robustly defended its independence at home and abroad. Sir Anthony Eden's Conservative government justified the military attack on the Canal Zone on the grounds that Egypt had ignored the ultimatum it had been given.

At the same time Eden's government was getting increasingly impatient at what it regarded as the disloyal attitude of the BBC. A cabinet committee was given the remit to decide whether the government was getting good value for money out of the World Service, and pressure was put on the BBC to persuade it that it should not be obsessed by its charter of impartiality. The BBC consequently found itself in a difficult position. Downing Street was seething. Some members of Eden's staff were making all sorts of wild threats about taking over the BBC. The real threat related to the World Service and whether it was being impartial in the way it projected British foreign policy abroad. Never before in BBC history had there been a crisis like this, in which a government was engaged in an operation overseas which did not have the wholehearted support of the entire British people, evidence of which was provided by a big demonstration that took place in London and elsewhere against the military action. But the BBC was trying to pursue its normal course of action, which was portraying the truth as it saw it, and giving both sides of the argument. While the BBC's worldwide reputation was enhanced by its protection of its charter of impartiality, the Suez Invasion effectively ended the political career of Sir Antony Eden, not only because of the failed seizure of the Suez Canal, but also by the later revelation that he had lied to parliament about the secret dealings with

France and Israel. Another consequence of this fiasco was that a very successful radio station in the heart of the Arab world ceased to exist.

My late brother Michael Kreitem, who served as an engineer in Sharq Al-Adna for more than forty-five years, recorded the following memories about Sharq Al-Adna looking at the station from a technical perspective:

Although there have been other publications of the history of Sharq Al-Adna and its fame in the Middle East, little has been written about it from the technical side.

Not many broadcasting stations existed in the Middle East in 1940 apart from local government stations radiating mainly in the medium wave band and most of them with low power transmitters, but they were effective, because there were few radiating in the band.

Sharq Al-Adna which meant Near East, or as it was announced in Arabic Mahatato Al-Sharq Aladna Lil-ithat Al-Arabia, started transmissions during the Second World War on a small scale in a little town north of Palestine, called Jenin, during the month of Ramadan in 1940. After a short while it moved to a building in the seaside town of Jaffa about 50 km north of Jerusalem. The studios consisted of one for continuity and another for production, and they were connected by Post Office music lines to the transmitter site 15 km south of Jerusalem to Bait-Jala near Bethlehem. The transmitters were sited on a hill overlooking Jerusalem. The building was not noticed from afar because it was surrounded by pine trees and the transmitter building was built semi underground and covered by camouflage netting. A similar dummy building was built on a nearby hill less than a mile away from the transmitter building as a decoy in case of air raids.

The transmitter building consisted of two halls, each accommodating two RCA 4750 type transmitters. In addition there was a small workshop and a power room with a standby engine and the station was powered from the mains supply. At the end of 1942, only two transmitters were on the air. At the same time, due to a shortage of transmitters, only one RCA 4750 type 7.5 kW was available, so two more transmitters were copied and made in the Palestine Post Office workshops in Jerusalem, even the modulation and HT transmitters were made by a local firm.

The Bait-Jala transmitting station was run by Arab and Jewish engineers from the Palestine Post Office. At the end of 1942, although there were four 4750 transmitters installed, only two were complete. One transmitter, an original RCA 4750 (locally made) transmitter, was radiating the Sharq Al-Adna programmes originated in the Jaffa studios. The second 4750 (locally made) transmitter was radiating European language programmes for the War Department, beamed to Europe. The programmes were originated in Jerusalem from a studio situated next to St Pierre Church just outside the walls of the old city of Jerusalem. Different European languages were transmitted on short wave and frequency changes were made every 15 minutes. Because of the War Department the Bait-Jala transmitting site was "hush-hush" and was well secured by troops of the Arab Legion from Transjordan. Programmes from St Pierre studios to Bait-Jala were also carried on Post Office music lines.

During the war the station was run by Post Office engineers, but was under military control. The chief engineer was Major Massey and his deputy was Captain Dixie Dean. In 1942 Sharq Al-Adna programmes radiated on 7.5 kW short-wave transmitter. Later two more 4750 7.5 kW transmitters were put on air, both on short wave. Sometime in 1943, Tim Hafferan, a sergeant in the Royal Signals, brought to the site a small transmitter and so the British Forces transmission (FBS) was started from Bait-Jala, programmes being originated also from St Pierre in Jerusalem. Later in the forties FBS built a separate building on the same site and installed an RCA 7.5 kW transmitter operating on the medium wave. The station then was run by engineers from the Royal Signals.

During the war there was also a small Hallicrafters transmitter in Bait-Jala radiating facsimile transmissions on short wave. At the end of the war, in March 1945, the Military Establishment HQ ME 18 officially took over the station and the original Post Office engineers returned to their former duties at the Palestinian Broadcasting Station. Arab and Jewish staff were employed to work with the ME 18 Engineers, and a captain of the Royal Signals (P. McGaw) became engineer in charge of Bait-Jala. Major Dean became the chief engineer of Sharq Al-Adna. The War Department European programmes ended and all four transmitters radiated Sharq Al-Adna programmes. Later its studios moved from Jaffa to Jerusalem, occupying ex-government buildings in Herod's Gate just outside the old walls of the city of Jerusalem near the Palestine Museum. But FBS continued their programmes from the studios at St Pierre.

During the war the Bait-Jala transmitters' engineers mostly lived in Jerusalem and were transported to the station in army trucks with canvas tops with wooden bench seats either side. Shift working hours were from 7 am to 7 am the next morning. Transmission hours were from 5 am till 11 pm, with a short break during the day. The shift workers used to sleep on site after transmission hours. Technical assistants used to be paid between £10 a month at the beginning of the war and about £25 a month by the end of the forties. After the war Sharq Al-Adna transport was similar but with wooden tops instead of canvas and the trucks used to bear the name of the station.

Sharq Al-Adna was well known in the Arab world and was getting more and more popular. At the end of the war local political troubles increased, but the station continued working. In 1947 the Jewish engineers found it difficult to go to work in Bait-Jala, which is an Arab town, but the station continued to function manned by about six Arab engineers, and that meant working overtime with little time to go home.

In about August 1947 plans to end the British Mandate in Palestine were under consideration, and so plans were made to move the station to an unknown place outside the country. Jewish engineers who could not report for duty were given small transmitters to install in army trucks ready for use on the new site, but when the work on them was about to be completed they were stolen by the Jewish underground terrorist organisation. In the meantime, plans to move the station continued.

In a letter addressed to all staff in October 1947 the director, Mr F.W. Benton, wrote: "On the occasion of his retirement, Colonel Hodgkin received from London a letter of warm commendation in which the whole of the station was involved. I am sure you will all be gratified to know that this said, among other things, that Sharq Al-Adna's standard in programme material and transmission was extremely high and had no way been adversely affected by the present difficult conditions in Palestine. Although there were four 4750 transmitters installed, only two were complete." The letter went on to say that this reflected the highest credit on the small staff who had in the past and present shown so much devotion both as regards simplicity of the organisation and operative effectiveness almost unequalled in the broadcasting world. The director was unable to give definite information about the future of the station. The letter was passed to the chief engineer who was A.W. Dean, who in turn sent it to Mr McGaw on 15 October 1947. In December 1947, in a letter headed "Near East Arab Broadcasting Station", the chief engineer said: "It has been decided that the station should if at all possible continue working in another location after the evacuation of the British Administration from Palestine. The new location had not finally been decided upon and he would like to take a certain number of the engineers to the new site."

So planning work to move the station was in hand. Three UK engineers were engaged to work on the new site: Harry Rowe, Harry Oakley and Dennis Fletcher. They came to Palestine for a brief visit and then went to Cyprus to start the installation of small transmitters to take over the service. That was early in 1948 and the first engineers from Bait-Jala station also went to Cyprus. These were diesel engineer Serob Karajanian, who went to organise power generation, and studio engineer K. Abogosh. Two more engineers also went to Cyprus to start working on the studios and they were Tim Heffernan and J. Brammel. As soon as the small transmitters in Cyprus were on the air, the Bait-Jala 4750 transmitters were dismantled and packed, and engineers

S. Shahi, M. Kreitem, E. Qamar and M. Abo Saad left Palestine on 5 April 1948. The situation was very tense, and they were asked to find their own way to the central bus station in Jerusalem. A 30-seater bus was organised to take them to Haifa, together with some of the programme staff. One soldier of the Transjordan Army accompanied the staff for security, and he was armed with a rifle. The atmosphere on route from Jerusalem to Haifa was very tense and fingers crossed that this soldier would not make a mistake while crossing any of the Jewish settlements. The staff slept one night in Haifa whilst all night shooting was going on. The following day, 6 April, they boarded the *Fouadieh* an Egyptian ship sailing between Alexandria, Haifa and Limassol, and arrived in Cyprus the next day, 7 April 1948.

The Bait-Jala staff started work at the new transmitter site in Limassol which was at Hippodromia, which in Greek means "Horse Racing Field". Small transmitters were installed in a small wooden hut, with a diesel engine in the open field supplying electricity because Limassol was then DC and privately owned. A big tent was used as a rest room. At Polemidia, which was part of the Cyprus Army Camp, one of the cars had been converted into a studio, and nearby was a wooden hut accommodating the programme staff. A transmitter site building for the second phase was completed, as well as two buildings as stores and an office, and during 1948 two 4750 transmitters went on the air. In the meantime the third phase was begun to build a proper stone building to accommodate four 4750 7.5 kW transmitters. This was completed about 1950. Aerial masts were all wooden, about 100 feet high, plus one tree. To upload the poles from the ship in Limassol they were thrown in the sea and fished out near the start of the present bypass and transported to Hippodromia. A power house was also built. At that time Sharq Al-Adna was the only broadcasting station in Cyprus. Later FBS started up in Dhekelia.

In the Middle East, few transmitters were in Jerusalem with one on medium wave, Damascus with two medium and four short wave, Cairo two medium and two short wave, Beirut one medium and two short, Baghdad one medium and one short, and Saudi Arabia from Mecca with one medium and five short. Later in the fifties stations in the Middle East started to grow in power and in frequencies. As a result Sharq with 4 x 7.5 kW short-wave transmitters started to be interfered with by adjacent channels and neighbouring countries were complaining of bad reception.

In January 1953 Sharq Al-Adna started to radiate on medium wave 635 KH (472 metres) from one of the 4750 transmitters which was modified from short to medium wave.

At Polemidia, nine stone buildings were built to accommodate studios and different departments; they included the director of the programme, organiser, studios, record library, newsroom, transport and a workshop. Soon after the beginning of 1948, the programme section started to bring over their staff, but the station orchestra and singers were not invited until a year later. They stayed in Cyprus for a few years and then moved to Beirut.In the early fifties, offices were opened in Cairo, Beirut, Amman and Baghdad – all were feeding Limassol with programmes. Most recordings were made on aluminum discs, which required trained recording engineers, but in the early fifties magnetic tapes started to be used, making life easier for the engineers and the programme staff. Studio equipment was mostly manufactured at the

Polemidia workshop and equipment was also sent to the mainland offices. The studio at Polemidia consisted of two continuity studios and one control room and in the same building there was a production studio large enough to accommodate the station orchestra. Opposite the studio building was the Newsroom, a well-organised section. News was received from different sources: Reuter was received on printers and neighbouring stations' news bulletins were monitored and recorded. The Arab news agency was also received in Arabic by Morse operators and it is worth mentioning that up to 1950 news bulletins were recorded on wax cylinders by 'Dictaphone' recorders which used to cut grooves on wax cylinders. When the recording was no longer required it was erased by turning it down on the lathe. Later in the fifties 'Dictorel' magnetic sheets were used for recording.

Near the news building there was a rich record library with the voices of kings and other great people of the Middle East, as well as many recordings specially made for Sharq Al-Adna. When Sharq closed down in 1956 some of the recordings, like Quran recitals, were dubbed onto tape and sent to the UK. This was organised by Mr Harding, an Arabist and archaeologist. The rest of the library was stored at the Zighy transmitter site and later destroyed.

After 1953 the station decided to increase the power of its transmitters. Hippodromia was a small site, and it was already causing interference in Limassol, even with 7.5 kW transmitters, and the programmes of Sharq used to be heard in the background of public address and other audio equipment. Plans to find a suitable site outside Limassol were going on. Lady's Mile was on the list, among other sites. Finally Zighy, 20 miles north of

Limassol, was selected. To prove that the site was good, a caravan with a small transmitter and a Phillips recorder was taken to the site, and test transmissions were radiated for a few nights. (D. Fletcher and M. Kreitem used to start the transmitter after 11 pm at Zighy.) So Zighy was built, and one Marconi 100 kW medium frequency with two 20 kW and two 7.5 kW short-wave transmitters were installed by G. Appleton and P. Rothery in 1955. Later Hippodromia closed down, and three of the 4750 transmitters were installed at Zighy – one radiated the BBC World Service on medium wave, the second was modified to medium wave and carried the BFBS programmes which used to come from Dhekelia via CYTA line, and the third 4750 transmitter was a standby for the new short-wave transmitters.

In 1953 Sharq Al-Adna became the first station in the Middle East to introduce advertising, which was very successful and profitable. As in Palestine, Cyprus had its problems and troubles for independence. In a letter addressed to all staff at Zighy, Polemidia and Hippodromia on 14 October 1955 the managing director said: "The following is the text of a letter from London by Mr F. Vandal Hovel, which I pass on with great pleasure:

I have been instructed by the Board of Directors to inform you, and through you all the members of your staff in Limassol, that the Board have noted with admiration the way in which the whole staff have faced up to the recent disturbances in Cyprus. Their steadiness, loyalty and devotion to duty is a splendid example of the team spirit and esprit-de-corps which characterise Sharq Al-Adna. The present troubles may yet continue until a good sense once more reigns in the Island, but the Board are confident that this spirit will carry Sharq Al-Adna through and that it can count, as in the past, on everyone's full cooperation. Will you, therefore, please tell all your staff that their bearing in these difficult times is keenly appreciated and that their example is an inspiration to all."

It is worth mentioning that Mr F. Vandal Hovel was one of the directors in London who came to Cyprus in 1955 on a fact-finding mission and was presented as Director of Near East Arab Broadcasting Station Ltd.

In November 1956 Sharq Al-Adna came to an end as the Suez Canal was bombed by the British and French forces who colluded with Israel. A few diplomatic wireless service engineers were at Polemidia, and there was an immediate need for Arab announcers to broadcast in Voice of Britain which took over from Sharq Al-Adna. A number of UK army officers who spoke Arabic were brought to attend voice tests but none were good enough to pass the tests because of their accent. By the time a few Arabs came from the mainland and started the Voice of Britain. News and commentary were unusual to the listeners to hear anti-Nasser propaganda. At the same time special transmissions in Arabic were recorded for replay and originated from a special studio in UK. This development came as a result of the requisition of Sharq Al-Adna by the British Governor of Cyprus before its independence.

In March 1957 Voice of Britain closed down and the Diplomatic Wireless Service officially took over the transmitter sites, and were used by the BBC Arabic Service as well as the English World Service. And they benefited and became more popular in the Middle East especially as their programmes were relayed on medium wave throughout the Middle East and beyond. Later on this service expanded, with new transmitters in Malta and Berbera, and reception furthered improve through broadcasting on FM.

The last transmitter which originated from Palestine was dismantled from Zighy in 1979. But the main entrance doors at Zighy still bear the name Sharq Al-Adna in artistic Arabic style.

Michel Kreitem. February 1982.